T0348524

Portfolio Management in Practice

Essential Capital Markets

Books in the series:

Portfolio Management in Practice

Christine Brentani

ELSEVIER
BUTTERWORTH
HEINEMANN

AMSTERDAM BOSTON HEIDELBERG LONDON NEW YORK OXFORD
PARIS SAN DIEGO SAN FRANCISCO SINGAPORE SYDNEY TOKYO

Elsevier Butterworth-Heinemann
Linacre House, Jordan Hill, Oxford OX2 8DP
200 Wheeler Road, Burlington, MA 01803

First published 2004

Copyright © 2001, Intellexis plc. All rights reserved
Additional material copyright © 2004, Elsevier Ltd. All rights reserved

No part of this publication may be reproduced in any material form (including
photocopying or storing in any medium by electronic means and whether
or not transiently or incidentally to some other use of this publication) without
the written permission of the copyright holder except in accordance with the
provisions of the Copyright, Designs and Patents Act 1988 or under the terms of
a licence issued by the Copyright Licensing Agency Ltd, 90 Tottenham Court Road,
London, England W1T 4LP. Applications for the copyright holder's written
permission to reproduce any part of this publication should be addressed
to the publisher

Permissions may be sought directly from Elsevier's Science and
Technology Rights Department in Oxford, UK: phone: (+44) (0) 1865 843830;
fax: (+44) (0) 1865 853333; e-mail: permissions@elsevier.co.uk. You may also
complete your request on-line via the Elsevier homepage
(www.elsevier.com), by selecting 'Customer Support' and then 'Obtaining
Permissions'

British Library Cataloguing in Publication Data
A catalogue record for this book is available from the British Library

Library of Congress Cataloguing in Publication Data
A catalogue record for this book is available from the Library of Congress

ISBN 0 7506 5906 8

For information on all Elsevier Butterworth-Heinemann finance
publications visit our website at: http://books.elsevier.com/finance

Printed and bound by CPI Group (UK) Ltd, Croydon, CR0 4YY
Transferred to Digital Print 2012

To Alex and Benjamin

Contents

Preface

It has often been said that portfolio management is not a science, but an art. Certainly, the human factor manifesting in a portfolio manager's ability to create outperformance bears out this truism. Computer systems can pick and run, to some extent, portfolios which will provide a return equal to an index, but the possibilities of higher fund outperformance (and under-performance) are presented by actively managed funds. With the more actively managed funds, portfolio managers can demonstrate their experience and expertise in picking assets, countries, sectors and companies that will generate positive returns.

This book was written to provide an overview of the day-to-day aspects with which a portfolio manager must be concerned. Theories and essential calculations are covered, along with a practical description of what is involved in managing portfolios. This book is not designed to focus on portfolio management in either a bull or a bear market scenario. Whether markets go up or down, the essential principles and methodologies of fund management hold true. Portfolio management has become an established means for managing investments, and is likely to continue gaining in strength as a way for savers to invest over the next decades.

Introduction

The single most prominent factor that has spurred the growth of portfolio management globally has been demographics. As more and more people across the developed world live longer, accumulate more wealth and have progressively higher standards of living, the need for financial security for the ageing population becomes vital. Increasingly, governments are withdrawing from the responsibility of providing retirement benefits to individuals, leading to a reduction in the welfare system. Corporations are also diminishing their role in the provision of retirement benefits to their employees. Individuals themselves are becoming more accountable for their own financial well-being after retirement. And trends that start in developed countries are often later replicated in the developing world. Thus, portfolio management as a vehicle for increasing personal wealth is set to continue in an expansionary phase.

Granted, markets go up and down, and individuals' inclinations towards investments in certain assets such as in bonds or in equities fluctuate over time. Nonetheless, portfolios or funds of pooled assets remain a means by which both individuals and institutions can, over time, enhance the returns on their savings. The choices of types of funds in which to invest are also continually evolving as markets change and as innovative products surface and are incorporated into new categories of funds.

The goal of portfolio management is to bring together various securities and other assets into portfolios that address investor needs, and then to manage those portfolios in order to achieve investment objectives. Effective asset management revolves around a portfolio manager's ability to assess and effectively manage risk. With the explosion of technology, access to information has increased dramatically at all levels of the investment cycle. It is the job of the portfolio manager to manage the vast array of available information and to transform it into successful investments for the portfolio for which he/she has the remit to manage.

This book reviews the main aspects of portfolio management. Both the theoretical and the practical sides of portfolio management are covered. The first part of the book will focus on the theoretical underpinnings of portfolio management. Investment management includes the formation of an optimal portfolio of assets, the determination of the best risk–return opportunities available from investment portfolios, and the choice of the best portfolio from that feasible set for a particular customer. Ways of measuring returns of existing portfolios will also be assessed. The second part of the book will review the types of securities and assets from which portfolio managers can choose in order to construct portfolios, and will also depict the wide variety of portfolios that can be created once client risk tolerance levels have been assessed. Different valuation methodologies will also be introduced. Although most of the book is devoted to equity investment, some characteristics of bond portfolio management will also be addressed.

Chapter 1

Managing portfolios

The most vital decision regarding investing that an investor can make involves the amount of risk he or she is willing to bear. Most investors will want to obtain the highest return for the lowest amount of possible risk. However, there tends to be a trade-off between risk and return, whereby larger returns are generally associated with larger risk. Thus, the most important issue for a portfolio manager to determine is the client's tolerance to risk. This is not always easy to do as attitudes toward risk are personal and sometimes difficult to articulate. The concept of risk can be difficult to define and to measure. Nonetheless, portfolio managers must take into consideration the riskiness of portfolios that are recommended or set up for clients.

This chapter assesses some of the constraints facing investors. An analysis of risk will be covered in the next chapter. Also, the main players in the money management business are reviewed. Investment institutions manage and hold at least 50% of the bond and equity markets in countries such as the USA and the UK. Thus, these institutions collectively can wield much influence over the money management industry, and potentially over stock and bond prices and even over company policies. The importance of one or another type of institutional money manager will vary from country to country. Finally, this chapter describes the most important investment vehicles available to these players.

Constraints

The management of customer portfolios is an involved process. Besides assessing a customer's risk profile, a portfolio manager must also take into account other considerations, such as the tax status of the investor and of the type of investment vehicle, as well as the client's resources, liquidity needs and time horizon of investment.

Resources

One obvious constraint facing an investor is the amount of resources available for investing. Many investments and investment strategies will have minimum requirements. For example, setting up a margin account in the USA may require a minimum of a few thousand dollars when it is established. Likewise, investing in a hedge fund may only be possible for individuals who are worth more than one million dollars, with minimum investments of several hundred thousand dollars. An investment strategy will take into consideration minimum and maximum resource limits.

Tax status

In order to achieve proper financial planning and investment, taxation issues must be considered by both investors and investment managers. In some cases, such as UK pension funds, the funds are not taxed at all. For these gross funds, the manager should attempt to avoid those stocks that include the deduction of tax at source. Even though these funds may be able to reclaim the deducted tax, they will incur an opportunity cost on the lost interest or returns they could have collected had they not had the tax deducted. Investors will need to assess any trade-offs between investing in tax-fee funds and fully taxable funds. For example, tax-free funds may have liquidity constraints meaning that investors will not be able to take their money out of the funds for several years without experiencing a tax penalty.

The tax status of the investor also matters. Investors in a higher tax category will seek investment strategies with favourable tax treatments. Tax-exempt investors will concentrate more on pretax returns.

Liquidity needs

At times, an investor may wish to invest in an investment product that will allow for easy access to cash if needed. For example, the investor may be considering buying a property within the next twelve months, and will want quick access to the capital. Liquidity considerations must be factored into the decision that determines what types of investment products may be suitable for a particular client. Also, within any fund there must be the ability to respond to changing circumstances, and thus a degree of liquidity must be built into the fund. Highly liquid stocks or fixed-interest instruments can guarantee that a part of the investment portfolio will provide quick access to cash without a significant concession to price should this be required.

Time horizons

An investor with a longer time horizon for investing can invest in funds with longer-term time horizons and can most likely stand to take higher risks, as poor returns in one year will most probably be cancelled by high returns in future years before the fund expires. A fund with a very short-term horizon may not be able to take this type of risk, and hence the returns may be lower. The types of securities in which funds invest will be influenced by the time horizon constraints of the funds, and the type of funds in which an investor invests will be determined by his or her investment horizon.

Special situations

Besides the constraints already mentioned, investors may have special circumstances or requirements that influence their investment universe. For example, the number of dependants and their needs will vary from investor to investor. An investor may need to plan ahead for school or university fees for one or several children. Certain investment products will be more suited for these investors. Other investors may want only to invest in socially responsible funds, and still other investors, such as corporate insiders or political officeholders, may be legally restricted regarding their investment choices.

Types of investors

Investors are principally categorized as either retail investors, who are private individuals with savings, or institutional investors, which include banks, pension funds and insurance companies.

Retail investors

Many retail investors do not have the time, skill or access to information to assess the many investment opportunities open to them and to manage their money in the most effective manner (although, with the abundance of financial and company information now available on the Internet, more individuals are taking the control of their financial management into their own hands). In practice, few individuals have sufficient money to build up a portfolio which diversifies risk properly. As a result, a variety of organizations, all professional intermediaries or middlemen, have developed a range of investment products and services for retail investors. These organizations range from small, independent firms of financial advisers (IFAs) who advise investors on how best to invest their funds in return for commissions from major financial organizations, to larger institutions such as banks, life assurance companies, fund management groups and stockbrokers.

By pooling individual investors' funds in various collective investment schemes, these intermediaries can (i) offer good returns at relatively low levels of risk; (ii) utilize the services of full-time, professional fund managers with access to the latest information; (iii) offer economies of scale in managing and administering the funds; (iv) minimize risk by investing in large, well diversified portfolios; and (v) depending on the particular product, provide a reasonable degree of liquidity, enabling the investor to buy or sell investments easily.

High net worth individuals will generally have more investment options available and can obtain specialized money management services. The professionals managing retail investor money or private client funds can offer the following services:

- **Execution only service**, which does not involve any advice or recommendations to the client but simply offers the means to buy and sell securities or assets for a commission. Very often, experienced financial investors who have the time and expertise to manage their own investment portfolios will choose this route.
- **Advisory dealing service**, which involves the stockbroker executing the business on behalf of the client, but also providing necessary advice regarding the transactions.
- **Portfolio advisory service**, whereby a stockbroker will assess the client's overall financial situation and needs and will provide advice on portfolio construction and investment strategy. However, it will be the client who gives the final word on the execution of the strategy.
- **Portfolio discretionary service**, where the stockbroker is responsible for the client's portfolio and is free to buy and sell assets on behalf of the client according to market conditions and other limitations that have been pre-arranged.

The objectives and structure of private client funds will vary depending on the needs and circumstances of the client. Generally, younger clients can afford to take more risk in their portfolios given their longer investment time horizon. Retired clients will most likely take less risk in their portfolios in order to preserve principal and income. For example, a younger retail investor may require life assurance-linked savings products to facilitate a house purchase, while older investors may seek high-yielding gilts and certain equity-related products to provide income and protection against inflation during their retirement.

Institutional investors

Similar to retail or private clients, many institutions or corporations, large and small, can decide to outsource the management of their proprietary Treasury portfolios, company pension schemes, or client portfolios to a third party. Institutional clients are particularly attractive to professional money management organizations, as they usually represent long-term relationships with clients who invariably possess a large volume of assets. As with private clients, the services that can be provided to institutional clients range from execution-only to full discretionary services. Institutional investors also include charities and other organizations such as certain universities, colleges and church commissioners.

The outsourcing of money management to external organizations has led to the growth of the consultant business. Consultants act as intermediaries helping institutions to select appropriate external money managers. The process usually involves assessing a parade of potential money managers' investment philosophies and styles, fee structures, past performances, personnel, and systems. The financial institutions contending for the business often have to fill out questionnaires and give presentations to the company outsourcing. The consultants will help develop the criteria by which the contenders are judged and will summarize the weaknesses and strengths of each for their client. In the end, the outsourcing company will make the final choice of which group it would like to manage its money and will then become that company's institutional client.

Banks

The core business of banks and building societies is to collect deposits and lend the money at a higher rate of interest. To optimize the return on these deposits banks invest in a range of money market and debt instruments, ranging from short-term Treasury bills to certificates of deposit to gilts and bonds, each with differing maturity profiles and liquidity. Since (in general terms) the longer the maturity the higher the rate of interest, sophisticated techniques are used by banks in order to create their desired portfolios and manage their assets/liabilities efficiently.

Many banks are also in the business of offering portfolio management alternatives to their retail clients. Retail investors may opt to keep part of their savings in unit trusts instead of in deposit accounts, particularly during periods where interest rates are low and stock market indices are rising. The managing of high net worth individual money (wealth management) is also a growth business for banks, and banks can offer institutional clients money management services. Over the years, investment management has been considered a growth business for banks, particularly in Europe. Portfolio management is a service that can be offered to existing clients in order to retain them as bank clients, and as a springboard for cross-selling other products to them. Money management services can also be used to acquire new clients. In all, portfolio management is considered a good fee-earning business for banks.

Insurance companies

Insurance companies bear risk. In return for receiving a set premium payment on a set schedule from the policyholder, the insurance company will pay out a predetermined amount to settle a claim if a specified event happens. The premiums are invested until a claim is made on the policy.

Insurance company activities can be divided into two categories: general insurance business and life assurance business. General insurance business offers insurance cover against specific contingencies such as fire, accident and motor insurance. These policies are normally reviewed annually. Liabilities from this type of insurance business are usually short term in nature, since most claims are made immediately after a relevant event has taken place. Thus the bulk of the funds of these general insurance companies is invested in cash and short-term debt instruments to match these short-term liabilities, with the balance invested in equities to achieve long-term growth.

Life assurance and, increasingly, permanent health insurance are mainly concerned with long-term business. Premiums are received from customers and these are invested and paid out to meet claims or when policies mature. The principal event, if insured against, is the death of the policyholder, in which case a lump sum will be paid to the deceased's estate or to a bank or building society in order to pay off a mortgage if the policy has been thus assigned. Life assurance policies can be categorized as follows:

- **Term assurance policies**, where the life of an individual is covered over a specified period (usually ten years or more). If the individual survives the period, no payment is made.
- **Whole life policies**, where a policyholder's life is insured until his or her death, whenever the death occurs.
- **Endowment policies**, where, in return for regular premiums, the policy will pay a fixed lump sum of money when a policyholder dies, or the same lump sum if a policyholder survives a pre-specified period of time.

Since insurance policies normally run for ten, twenty or more years, the funds tend to be invested predominantly in equities in order to provide long term growth in income and capital, combined with protection against inflation. The balance of the funds is usually invested in gilts.

The investment returns of life fund businesses are subject to both capital gains tax and income tax, and as a result life assurance portfolio managers will adjust their investment strategies accordingly to minimize the tax paid on their funds. Life assurance premiums are paid net of tax by policyholders.

Insurance companies in the UK are tightly regulated by the Department of Trade and Industry and may be restricted from investing in certain types of assets.

Pension funds

A pension scheme is a fund established to pay pension benefits to beneficiaries upon their retirement. A pension scheme is normally set up by an employer in an effort to attract or retain employees, but may be set up by local councils for their employees, unions or trade associations, or even by private individuals for themselves (normally referred to as pension plans).

Two main types of pension funds are prominent:

- **Defined benefit**, where the sponsor agrees to pay members of the scheme a pension equal to a predetermined percentage of their final salary subject to the number of years which the contributor has worked
- **Defined contribution** where contributions are used to buy investments and it is the return on these investments that will determine the pension benefits.

Contributions are made by employers and/or employees into the scheme, and these are then invested in order to build up a capital sum and to generate an income out of which pensions and other benefits are paid. The management of pension schemes may be wholly or partially delegated to fund managers, including banks, fund management groups or even life assurance companies.

The usual principal objectives of pension funds are to achieve the maximum rate of return in excess of inflation over the long term, to maintain a surplus (i.e. an excess of assets over projected liabilities calculated on an actuarial basis), and to be able to meet their liabilities as they fall due.

The investment policies of both private and institutional investors will be partially determined by their tax status. Pension funds are exempt from both income and capital gains tax, and contributions to a pension scheme are not taxable. Generally, pension funds have fairly long-term time horizons and are thus able to take on more risk. As a result, these types of funds can invest in slightly more speculative assets, such as equities and property with a smaller proportion invested in fixed interest securities.

Fund management companies

Fund management companies comprise another significant category of investment management player. These companies may be subsidiaries of banks, part of stockbroking groups, or independent companies that manage funds for retail investors and for institutional investors, including pension funds, insurance companies and charities.

Some institutional investors employ their own fund managers and outsource specialized parts of their portfolios, such as Japanese stocks, private equity or emerging markets, to specialist fund managers at fund management companies. Many small and medium sized pension funds completely subcontract the role of fund management to fund management companies.

Investment vehicles

Most investment management players will offer their clients collective investment schemes known as unit trusts and investment trusts. (Alternative investment vehicles, such as hedge funds and private equity, are also an option for certain qualified players). With these products, the professional money manager manages larger funds comprised of money pooled from a large number of smaller investors.

Unit trusts

A unit trust is an open-ended fund in which investors buy units representing their proportional share of the assets and income in the trust. The money invested in the fund is used to buy shares or bonds, depending on the investment objective of the unit trust. A unit trust is constituted under a Trust Deed between a fund manager and an independent trustee, usually a bank or large insurance company. The trust is not a separate legal entity but actually a legal relationship between the trustee as the legal owner of the trust's assets (usually shares and/or bonds) and the investors who will benefit.

Units may be either income units (on which the trust's income is paid out periodically) or accumulation units (where income is not paid out but is added to capital in the form of new units). As an open-ended fund, more units can be issued when investors want to buy or the number reduced when investors want to redeem. In the former case new investments in the fund can be purchased, and in the latter investments have to be sold. The price of each unit reflects the current value of the fund divided by the number of outstanding units.

In the UK and in certain other European countries, unit trusts are limited in the amount they can invest in any one security. Up to 10% of the fund may be invested in the shares of a single company up to the level of four such investments (i.e. 40% of the fund). After reaching this level, the fund can only invest 5% of the value of the fund in any further single investment. Another rule states that a unit trust may not hold more than 10% of the total voting share capital issued by a single company. Unit trusts tend to charge an annual management fee that is fixed as a percentage of the value of the fund. In some countries, such as in the UK, investors purchase units at an offer price and sell the units back to the unit trust manager at a lower bid price.

In the USA, the equivalent investment vehicle to a unit trust is a mutual fund. A mutual fund is a corporation owned by its shareholders. The shareholders elect a board of directors, who are responsible for hiring a manager to oversee the fund's operations. Most mutual funds are created by mutual fund companies (also known as investment advisory firms). These firms may offer other financial services, such as discount brokerage as well as fund management.

Investment trusts

Another investment vehicle offered by money managers is the investment trust. First founded in the 1860s, investment trusts are companies specifically set up to invest in the shares of other companies. They offer both corporate and individual private investors a way to purchase a diversified portfolio of securities. Investment trusts are not trusts, but limited liability companies. All investment trusts are listed on the Stock Exchange (but not all investment companies are). An investment trust has a fixed number of shares, and is known as a closed end fund. It has a fixed capital structure, and can only raise more capital by having a rights issue or by borrowing. The share price is determined solely by supply and demand, and may not mirror the performance of the underlying investments made by the trust. Where the net asset value per share is higher than the share price, the share price stands at a discount to net asset value. In the reverse case, the share price trades at a premium to the net asset value of the investment trust.

An investment trust is managed by a board of directors, who determine the investment trust's investment strategy, which is then carried out by the management of the investment trust. The objective of the investment trust's board is to maximize the value of the investments and share price for its shareholders. The rules governing the activities of the investment trust state that a maximum of 15% of the trust can be invested in a single company. In addition, the managers of the investment trust will charge an annual fee for their management services.

Generally, the main form of share capital in which investment trusts invest are ordinary shares paying out income in the form of regular dividends and offering the possibility of a capital gain. Investment trusts that have more than one main class of share are called split capital trusts. These trusts will have at least two classes of shares that meet the needs of different investors. They are designed to split capital from income. Split capital trusts are structured to have a predetermined date for winding up and, until that date, the right to dividends and the right to capital growth are split between each class of shares.

Open-ended investment companies

As of 1997 a new type of collective investment vehicle was created in the UK, called an open-ended investment company (OEIC). OEICs are similar to unit trusts in that they are available to the general public, the number of units or shares can vary from day to day, and their price will reflect the value of the fund's underlying portfolio. Also, they are subject to a similar regulatory regime as unit trusts. However, they resemble investment trusts in that they have a company structure, and the assets of the fund are overseen by a depository and not a trustee.

OEICs are meant to attract non-UK investors who are uncomfortable investing in the UK due to lack of experience with the trust concept. With OEICs, private investors will be allowed to move between different sub-funds under a single OEIC – for example from UK income to UK growth. This is cheaper than moving between unit trusts. Also, OEICs will be able to issue different classes of shares, which will facilitate different fee structures and allow for shares denominated in different currencies.

Quiz: Chapter 1

1 _____ have fairly long time horizons and are able to invest in more speculative assets.

   (A) General business insurance companies
   (B) Pension funds
   (C) Investment trusts
   (D) Commercial bank treasury departments
   (E) Pensioners

2 With _____ , the broker can have the final say on which assets are bought and sold in a portfolio.

   (A) execution only service
   (B) portfolio due diligence service
   (C) advisory dealing service
   (D) portfolio discretionary service
   (E) portfolio advisory service

3 _____ occur where a trust's income is not paid out, but added to the capital in the form of new units.

   (A) Accumulation units
   (B) Income units
   (C) Distribution units
   (D) Dividends
   (E) Taxes

4 In the UK _____ can invest up to 10% in the shares of a single company, whereas _____ can invest up to 15% in a single company.

   (A) pension funds, banks
   (B) investment trusts, unit trusts
   (C) banks, pension funds
   (D) insurance companies, pension funds
   (E) unit trusts, investment trusts

5 In the UK, a(n) _____ advises retail customers on financial matters.

(A) PIA

(B) IMRO

(C) IFA

(D) SIB

(E) SFA

6 With _____ pension systems, contributions are used to buy securities and other investments whereby the returns on those investments determine the pension benefits.

(A) OEIC

(B) defined benefit

(C) unit trust

(D) defined contribution

(E) term assurance

7 With a(n) _____ , the policyholder has his/her life insured regardless of when the death occurs.

(A) endowment policy

(B) term assurance policy

(C) OEIC policy

(D) investment policy

(E) whole life policy

Chapter 2

Portfolio theory

A discussion of portfolio or fund management must include some thought given to the concept of risk. Any portfolio that is being developed will have certain risk constraints specified in the fund rules, very often to cater to a particular segment of investor who possesses a particular level of risk appetite. It is, therefore, important to spend some time discussing the basic theories of quantifying the level of risk in an investment, and to attempt to explain the way in which market values of investments are determined.

Risk and risk aversion

Risk versus return is the reason why investors invest in portfolios. The ideal goal in portfolio management is to create an optimal portfolio derived from the best risk–return opportunities available given a particular set of risk constraints. To be able to make decisions, it must be possible to quantify the degree of risk in a particular opportunity. The most common method is to use the standard deviation of the expected returns. This method measures spreads, and it is the possible returns of these spreads that provide the measure of risk.

The presence of risk means that more than one outcome is possible. An investment is expected to produce different returns depending on the set of circumstances that prevail.

For example, given the following for Investment A:

Circumstance	Return (x)	Probability (p)
I	10%	0.2
II	12%	0.3
III	15%	0.4
IV	19%	0.1

It is possible to calculate:

1 *The expected (or average) return*
  Mean (average) = $\bar{x}$ = expected value (EV) = Σpx

Circumstance	Return (x)	Probability (p)		px
I	10%	0.2	=	2.0
II	12%	0.3	=	3.6
III	15%	0.4	=	6.0
IV	19%	0.1	=	1.9
		Expected return		13.5%
			=	Σpx

2 *The standard deviation*
  Standard deviation = $\sigma = \sqrt{\Sigma p(x-\bar{x})^2}$

Also, variance (VAR) is equal to the standard deviation squared or σ^2.

Circumstance	Return (x)	Probability (p)	Deviation from expected return (x–$\bar{x}$)	$p(x-\bar{x})^2$
I	10%	0.2	−3.5%	2.45
II	12%	0.3	−1.5%	0.68
III	15%	0.4	+1.5%	1.90
IV	19%	0.1	+5.5%	3.03
			Variance =	7.06

Standard deviation $(\sigma) = \sqrt{variance}$
$$= \sqrt{7.06}$$
$$= 2.66\%$$

The standard deviation is a measure of risk, whereby the greater the standard deviation, the greater the spread, and the greater the spread, the greater the risk.

If the above exercise were to be performed using another investment that offered the same expected return, but a different standard deviation, then the following result might occur:

	Expected return	*Risk (standard deviation)*
Investment A	9%	2.5%
Investment B	9%	4.0%

Since both investments have the same expected return, the best selection of investment would be Investment A, which provides the lower risk. Similarly, if there are two investments presenting the same risk, but one has a higher return than the other, that investment would be chosen over the investment with the lower return for the same risk.

In the real world, there are all types of investors. Some investors are completely risk averse and others are willing to take some risk, but expect a higher return for that risk. Different investors will also have different tolerances or threshold levels for risk–return trade-offs – i.e. for a given level of risk, one investor may demand a higher rate of return than another investor.

Indifference curves

Suppose the following situation exists:

	Expected return	*Risk (standard deviation)*
Investment A	10%	5%
Investment B	20%	10%

The question to ask here is, does the extra 10% return compensate for the extra risk? There is no right answer, as the decision would depend on the particular investor's attitude to risk. A particular investor's indifference curve can be ascertained by plotting what rate of return the investor would require for each level of risk to be indifferent amongst all of the investments. For example, there may be an investor who can obtain a return of £50 with zero risk and a return of £55 with a risk or standard deviation of £5 who will be indifferent between the two investments. If further investments were considered, each with a higher degree of risk, the investor would require still higher returns to make all of the investments equally attractive. The investor being discussed could present the following as the indifference curve shown in Figure 2.1:

Return	Risk
£50	£0
£55	£5
£70	£10
£100	£15
£120	£18
£230	£25

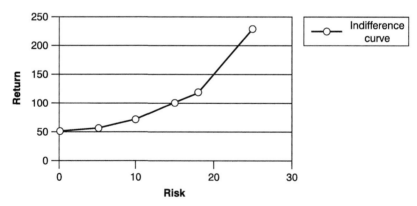

Figure 2.1 Indifference curve

It could be the case that this investor would have different indifference curves given a different starting level of return for zero risk. The exercise would need to be repeated for various levels of risk–return starting points. An entire set of indifference curves could be constructed that would portray a particular investor's attitude towards risk (see Figure 2.2).

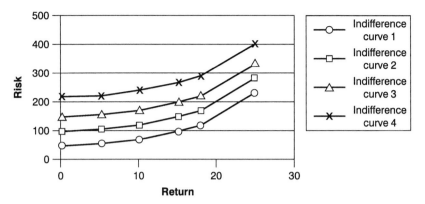

Figure 2.2 Indifference curves

Utility scores

At this stage the concept of utility scores can be introduced. These can be seen as a way of ranking competing portfolios based on the expected return and risk of those portfolios. Thus if a fund manager had to determine which investment a particular investor would prefer, i.e. Investment A equalling a return of 10% for a risk of 5% or Investment B equalling a return of 20% for a risk of 10%, the manager would create indifference curves for that particular investor and look at the utility scores. Higher utility scores are assigned to portfolios or investments with more attractive risk–return profiles. Although several scoring systems are legitimate, one function that is commonly employed assigns a portfolio or investment with expected return or value EV and variance of returns σ^2 the following utility value:

$$U = EV - .005A\sigma^2$$

where:

U = utility value

A = an index of the investor's aversion, (the factor of .005 is a scaling convention that allows expression of the expected return and standard deviation in the equation as a percentage rather than a decimal).

Utility is enhanced by high expected returns and diminished by high risk. Investors choosing amongst competing investment portfolios will select the one providing the highest utility value. Thus, in the example above, the investor will select the investment (portfolio) with the higher utility value of 18.

Expected return (EV)	Standard deviation (σ)	Utility $= EV - .005A\sigma^2$
10%	5%	$10 - .005 \times 4 \times 25 = 9.5$
20%	10%	$20 - .005 \times 4 \times 100 = 18$
		(Assume $A = 4$ in this case)

Portfolio diversification

There are several different factors that cause risk or lead to variability in returns on an individual investment. Factors that may influence risk in any given investment vehicle include uncertainty of income, interest rates, inflation, exchange rates, tax rates, the state of the economy, default risk and liquidity risk (the risk of not being able to sell on the investment). In addition, an investor will assess the risk of a given investment (portfolio) within the context of other types of investments that may already be owned, i.e. stakes in pension funds, life insurance policies with savings components, and property.

One way to control portfolio risk is via **diversification**, whereby investments are made in a wide variety of assets so that the exposure to the risk of any particular security is limited. This concept is based on the old adage 'do not put all your eggs in one basket'. If an investor owns shares in only one company, that investment will fluctuate depending on the factors influencing that company. If that company goes bankrupt, the investor might lose 100 per cent of the investment. If, however, the investor owns shares in several companies in different sectors, then the likelihood of all of those companies going bankrupt simultaneously is greatly diminished. Thus, diversification reduces risk. Although bankruptcy risk has been considered here, the same principle applies to other forms of risk.

Covariance and correlation

The goal is to hold a group of investments or securities within a portfolio potentially to reduce the risk level suffered without reducing the level of return. To measure the success of a potentially diversified portfolio, *covariance* and *correlation* are considered. Covariance measures to what degree the returns of two risky assets move in tandem. A positive covariance means that the returns of the two assets move together, whilst a negative covariance means that they move in inverse directions.

Covariance

$COV(x,y) = \Sigma p(x - \bar{x})(y - \bar{y})$ for two investments x and y, where p is the probability.

Covariance is an absolute measure, and covariances cannot be compared with one another. To obtain a relative measure, the formula for correlation coefficient [r] is used.

Correlation coefficient

$$r = \frac{COVxy}{\sigma_x \sigma_y}$$

To illustrate the above, here is an example:

Circumstance	Probability	$x - \bar{x}$	$y - \bar{y}$	$p(x-\bar{x})(y-\bar{y})$
I	0.2	+1.0	−3.5	−0.7
II	0.3	0	−1.5	0
III	0.4	+1.5	+1.5	0.9
IV	0.1	−4	+5.5	−2.2
			COV_{xy} =	−2.0

For data regarding $(y - \bar{y})$, see earlier example. Assume that a similar exercise has been run for data regarding $(x - \bar{x})$. Assume the variance or σ^2 of x = 2.45, and the variance or σ^2 of y = 7.06. Thus, the correlation coefficient would be:

$$r = \frac{-2.0}{\sqrt{2.45} \times \sqrt{7.056}} = -0.481$$

If the same example is run again, but using a different set of numbers for y, a different correlation coefficient might result of, say, −0.988. It can be concluded that a large negative correlation confirms the strong tendency of the two investments to move inversely.

Perfect positive correlation (correlation coefficient = +1) occurs when the returns from two securities move up and down together in proportion. If these securities were combined in a portfolio, the 'offsetting' effect would not occur.

Perfect negative correlation (correlation coefficient = –1) takes place when one security moves up and the other one down in exact proportion. Combining these two securities in a portfolio would increase the diversification effect.

Uncorrelated (correlation coefficient = 0) occurs when returns from two securities move independently of each other – that is, if one goes up, the other may go up or down or may not move at all. As a result, the combination of these two securities in a portfolio may or may not create a diversification effect. However, it is still better to be in this position than in a perfect positive correlation situation.

Unsystematic and systematic risk

As mentioned previously, diversification diminishes risk: the more shares or assets held in a portfolio or in investments, the greater the risk reduction. However, it is impossible to eliminate all risk completely even with extensive diversification. The risk that remains is called market risk; the risk that is caused by general market influences. This risk is also known as systematic risk or non-diversifiable risk. The risk that is associated with a specific asset and that can be abolished with diversification is known as unsystematic risk, unique risk or diversifiable risk.

Total risk = Systematic risk + Unsystematic risk

Systematic risk = the potential variability in the returns offered by a security or asset caused by general market factors, such as interest rate changes, inflation rate movements, tax rates, state of the economy.

Unsystematic risk = the potential variability in the returns offered by a security or asset caused by factors specific to that company, such as profitability margins, debt levels, quality of management, susceptibility to demands of customers and suppliers.

As the number of assets in a portfolio increases, the total risk may decline as a result of the decline in the unsystematic risk in that portfolio.

The relationship amongst these risks can be quantified as follows:

$$TR^2 = SR^2 + UR^2 \text{ or } \sigma_i^2 = \sigma_s^2 + \sigma_u^2$$

where:

σ_i = the investment's total risk (standard deviation)
σ_s = the investment's systematic risk
σ_u = the investment's unsystematic risk.

The correlation coefficient between two investment opportunities can be expressed as:

$$\sigma_s = \sigma_i COR_{im}$$

where:

σ_s = the investment's systematic risk
σ_i = the investment's total risk (systematic and unsystematic)
COR_{im} = the correlation coefficient between the returns of the investment and those of the market.

If an investment were perfectly correlated to the market so that all its movements could be fully explained by movements in the market, then all of the risk would be systematic and $\sigma_i = \sigma_s$. If an investment were not correlated at all to the market, then all of its risk would be unsystematic.

The efficient frontier

Given the following inputs – returns, standard deviations, and correlations – a minimum-variance portfolio for any targeted expected return can be calculated. For example, assume that for the given level of returns, the best portfolio for each had been calculated:

Return	*Risk of 'best' portfolio*
15%	0.22%
12%	0.19%
8%	0.23%
20%	0.40%
25%	0.55%

The data could be plotted as in Figure 2.3.

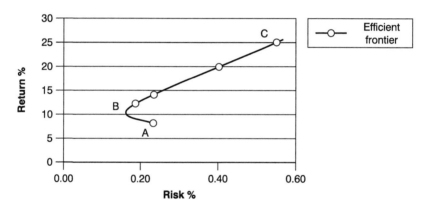

Figure 2.3 Efficient frontier

The part of the curve between points B and C (i.e. above point B, which is the point of global minimum variance) represents the efficient frontier, as this part of the curve represents the highest return possible for a given level of risk. The points on the curve between A and B produce a lower return for a higher risk than point B. Drawing on the previous section regarding indifference curves and utility values, the investor would prefer that investment or portfolio that lay furthest through the indifference curve.

In practice, it may be difficult to assess the various indifference curves and the efficient frontier for a particular investor. Fortunately, software programs known as quadratic optimization programs can help to calculate

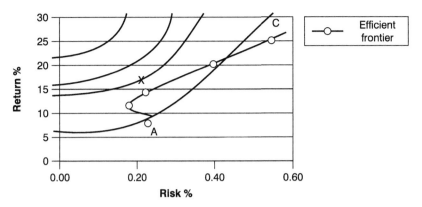

Figure 2.4 Efficient frontier and indifference curves

efficient sets of portfolios. If a portfolio manager is dealing with n (i.e. 50) securities, he or she will need n estimates of expected return, n estimates of variances and $(n^2 - n)/2$ (i.e. 1225) covariances.

The capital market line

Following the development of the efficient frontier of presumably risky assets, it is possible to combine this portfolio with a risk-free asset with a return of Rf and a risk of 0. The line with the highest reward to variability ratio (steepest slope) can be drawn, giving the graph shown in Figure 2.5.

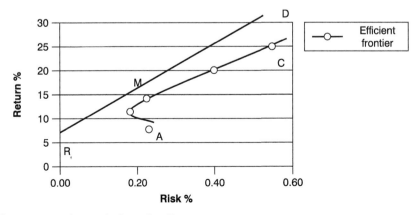

Figure 2.5 The capital market line

The efficient frontier is arrived at by considering risky investments in the original curve calculated ABC, and by introducing the risk-free investments. The efficient frontier is now the straight line. The assumption is that borrowing and lending are allowed. Thus, the line RfM assumes that an investor invests a portion of his or her investment in the risk-free investment and the rest in the risky portfolio M. The other section of the curve MD assumes that the investor can borrow at the risk-free rate and invest more than 100% of his or her investment in the market portfolio M. The line RfMD is the capital market line (CML). The equation for the CML is:

$$E(Rp) = \frac{Rf + E(Rm) - Rf}{\sigma_m} \times \sigma_p$$

where:

$E(Rp)$ = expected return given risk = σ_p
$E(Rm)$ = risk-free rate for portfolio m given risk = σ_m

Thus, for a portfolio on the CML, the expected rate of return in excess of the risk-free rate is proportional to the standard deviation of that portfolio.

To use an example: if the market return is 8%, the market standard deviation is 15%, and the risk-free return is 4.5%, what is the expected return on an efficient portfolio with a risk of 12%?

$$E(Rp) = 4.5 + \frac{8 - 4.5}{15} \times 12 = 7.3\%$$

The capital asset pricing model

According to the IIMR *Investment Management Certificate Official Training Manual* in the UK:

> The capital asset pricing model (CAPM) was developed in the early 1960s from modern portfolio theory by academic finance theorists. Although much maligned, the model remains as perhaps the most popular tool for quantifying and measuring risk for equities in academic circles and in the investment industry in the USA, but is less popular with the UK investment community. The main attraction of the CAPM is the simplicity

of its predictions. However, according to detractors of the model, the simplicity is achieved at the expense of a realistic view of how financial markets work.

The derivation of the model requires certain assumptions and simplifications about financial markets and investors. These assumptions are that:

1 Investors are risk averse and maximize expected utility
2 Investors choose portfolios or investments on the basis of their expected mean and variance of returns
3 Investors have a single-period time horizon that is the same for all investors
4 Borrowing and lending at the risk-free rate are unrestricted
5 Investor expectations regarding the means, variances and covariances of asset returns are homogeneous
6 There are no taxes and no transaction costs.

The security market line

The conclusion of the CAPM is known as the security market line (SML), and can be expressed as follows:

$$r_p = r_f + \beta(r_m - r_f)$$

where:

r_p = the expected return on asset or portfolio p
r_f = the return available from a risk-free asset (this could be the return on a government bill or bond)
r_m = the expected return on the market, such as the return on the FT All Share Index
β = measure of the sensitivity of the asset to the market (see below for further discussion).
$r_m - r_f$ = the market risk premium, or the excess return over the risk-free rate received by investing in a portfolio of risky assets. This figure has been coming down over the last few years, and is predicted to be lower over the next 100 years compared to the past 100 years.

The CAPM provides the framework to determine the relationship between expected return and risk for individual securities as well as for portfolios. The security market line shows that the expected return on a share is the sum of the risk-free return and the market risk premium adjusted for the relative volatility of the share.

One of the forecasts of the CAPM is that in equilibrium, all assets or portfolios lie on the security market line. If an investment lay above the SML it would be accepted by an investor as it is offering a return higher than that required for its level of risk (undervalued). If an investment lay below the SML, it would be rejected as its return is too low (undervalued).

Beta coefficient

The beta coefficient is a key factor of the CAPM, and can be written as:

$$\beta_p = \frac{COV\ (r_p,\ r_m)}{VAR\ (r_m)}$$

where

$COV\ (r_p,\ r_m)$ = the covariance of the return on portfolio p with the return on the market

$VAR\ (r_m)$ = the variance of the return on the market

Beta determines the relative sensitivity of the investment to the market. Another way of looking at the beta of an investment is that it is a relative measure of the systematic risk of that investment.

For a situation where $\beta > 1$, the investment will produce returns in the same direction as the market's, but to a larger extent.

When $\beta = 1$, the investment's returns should move in the same direction as the market's returns and by the same amount.

For situations where $0 < \beta < 1$, the investment will deliver returns in the same direction as the market's, but to a lesser degree. For example, a beta of 0.5 would mean that, on average, the investment's returns move half as much as the market's do (in the same direction), and could be considered less risky than investing in the market.

If $\beta = 0$, then the investment's returns are not correlated with those of the market. This could occur if the investment is risk free, or when all of the investment's risk is non-systematic.

When the beta is a negative number, this means that the investment's returns will move in the opposite direction to those of the market.

The following example illustrates CAPM:

Suppose the risk free rate of return is 5%, and the expected market return is 10%. What return will a diversified investor require from investments with betas of 0, 0.5, 1, and 1.5?

Again, the formula is: $r_p = r_f + \beta(r_m - r_f)$

so:

if $\beta = 0$, $\quad r_p = 5\% + 0 \times (10\% - 5\%) = 5\%$
if $\beta = 0.5$, $\quad r_p = 5\% + 0.5 \times (10\% - 5\%) = 7.5\%$
if $\beta = 1$, $\quad r_p = 5\% + 1 \times (10\% - 5\%) = 10.0\%$
if $\beta = 1.5$, $\quad r_p = 5\% + 1.5 \times (10\% - 5\%) = 12.5\%$

Where the beta $= 1$ the expected return of the investment is equal to the expected return on the market, and the higher the beta coefficient, the higher the expected return.

CAPM can be used for the formation of portfolios where the portfolio manager has determined the degree of risk that the client is willing to bear. An individual seeking a high return would take on more risk and a portfolio constructed using a higher beta. A young pension fund, for example, with a longer term horizon, may employ an investment strategy that would invest in a portfolio with a beta greater than 1. This portfolio could be expected to give returns greater than those of the market, but at a correspondingly higher level of risk. Likewise, a mature pension fund is more likely to seek a safer portfolio and would probably prefer a portfolio with a beta of less than 1. As the proportion of risk-free investments is increased in the portfolio and the proportion of equities decreased, the portfolio beta reduces towards 0. Using another example, if an investor wanted to buy units in a unit trust with a beta of 0.75, but no such fund existed, the investor could put 50% of the investment in a unit trust with a beta of 0.5 and the rest of the funds in a unit trust with a beta of 1.0. Holding both these funds replicates holding units in one unit trust with a beta of 0.75.

In a similar vein, if a new investment is added to a portfolio, the beta of the new portfolio will be the weighted average of the beta of the old portfolio and the new security. Thus:

$$\beta = \Sigma w_i \beta_i$$

where:

w_i = market value weighting of portfolio component i
β_i = the β of the portfolio constituent i.

For example, an existing portfolio of £50m has a beta of 0.75. A new investment of £5m with a beta of 1.2 is added to the portfolio. The new overall beta of the portfolio will therefore be:

$$0.75 \times \frac{£50m}{£55m} + 1.2 \times \frac{£5m}{£55m} = 0.79$$

Quiz: Chapter 2

1 What are the expected return and standard deviation, given the following data?

Circumstance	Return	Probability
I	10%	0.2
II	6%	0.5
III	4%	0.3

(A) 5.1%, 3.0%
(B) 6.2%, 1.96%
(C) 6%, 2.55%
(D) 6.2%, 3.88%
(E) 1.96%, 3.88%

2 Controlling risk in a portfolio by investing in a wide variety of assets is known as:

(A) Correlation
(B) Covariance
(C) Diversification
(D) Probability
(E) Variance

3 Assuming the following data, what is the correlation coefficient and how would this be interpreted?

Circumstance	Probability	$(x - \bar{x})$	$(y - \bar{y})$
I	0.2	−3.0	−1.5
II	0.5	+1.0	+0.8
III	0.3	+5.0	+2.5

Variance of x = 8.02
Variance of y = 2.30

(A) 0.961, very high positive correlation
(B) 0.121, very little correlation

(C) −0.961, very high negative correlation

(D) −0.121, very low negative correlation

(E) 0.690, some positive correlation

4 Market risk that remains in a portfolio and is impossible to diversify completely is also known as:

(A) Total risk

(B) Systematic risk

(C) Unsystematic risk

(D) Uncorrelated risk

(E) Company risk

5 A share has a beta of 1.3. If the risk-free rate is 5% and the market return is 15%, what is the expected return on the share?

(A) 15%

(B) 18%

(C) 5%

(D) 10%

(E) 13%

6 An existing £100 million portfolio has a beta of 1.5. A new investment of £50 million with a beta of 0.8 is added to this portfolio. What is the new beta of the portfolio?

(A) 1.5

(B) 1.0

(C) 1.7

(D) 0.7

(E) 1.3

Chapter 3

Measuring returns

Once a portfolio has been established, it is important to monitor the fund's performance. Measuring the performance of a portfolio involves calculating the returns achieved by the fund over a particular period of time, known as the evaluation period. The evaluation period used to monitor performance may be weekly, monthly, quarterly or annually. Various methods may be used to calculate returns, each giving a different result. Parties interested in evaluating performance use consistent and standard methods for calculating and presenting returns, several of which are reviewed below.

Performance evaluation involves comparing the performance of a fund against a suitable yardstick or benchmark (usually a relevant index) after adjusting for risk in order to determine how the fund manager has performed and how the returns were actually achieved. Evaluation enables the investor to check that the agreed investment strategy has been followed, and to assess the skill of the fund manager.

Calculating returns

Clients, trustees of pension funds and unit trusts, board of directors of investment trust companies and managers of fund management departments are amongst the groups interested in monitoring the capabilities of the fund managers and analysts who contribute to the running of the funds. Although calculating returns is simple in theory, it is relatively more complex in practice. The methods considered are money return, time-weighted return and money-weighted return.

Total return or money return

The first step in assessing performance is to measure the total return that a fund has produced. To calculate this return, the value of each share in the fund at the beginning of the evaluation period is multiplied by the number of shares held. The sum of these values is the market value of the portfolio at the beginning of the time period. The same procedure is carried out using the market prices and amounts of the holdings at the end of the time period to calculate the market value of the portfolio at the end of the evaluation period. The total return (also known as money return) from the portfolio is calculated as follows:

$$\text{Total return } r = \frac{V_{end} - V_{beginning}}{V_{beginning}}$$

where:

$V_{beginning}$ = market value of the fund at the beginning of the period
V_{end} = market value of the fund at the end of the period (including reinvested dividends or coupon payments).

If, for example, V_{end} is £5 million, $V_{beginning}$ is £4 million, calculate the money return:

$$r = \frac{£5 - £4}{£4} \times 100 = 25\%$$

The next step to examine is what happens when clients add new money to the fund or withdraw money from the fund. Money may be added or withdrawn at any time during the examination period. If the money is added just before the end of the period, the above formula would have to be adjusted as follows:

$$r = \frac{(V_{end} - D) - V_{beginning}}{V_{beginning}}$$

where:

V_{end} = the portfolio value at the end of the period
$V_{beginning}$ = the portfolio value at the beginning of the period
D = deposits into the fund by the investor.

For example, if V_{end} is £5 million, $V_{beginning}$ is £4 million and a cash input (D) of £250 000 is made, the money return is calculated as:

$$r = \frac{(£5 - £0.25) - £4}{£4} \times 100 = 12.5\%$$

If the cash input had not been subtracted, the return quoted would have been 25% rather than 12.5%. This would have been misleading, since part of the increase was due to money coming into the fund and not to the fund manager's skill. Withdrawals from a fund or distributions made from a fund to shareholders can also produce a distorting effect, and thus the timing of deposits into and withdrawals from a portfolio must be taken into account.

The above example assumes distributions into and out of the fund are made at the end of the period. This is unlikely to be true in practice, and the following two methods overcome the problem by breaking the evaluation period into smaller sub-periods.

Money-weighted returns

This technique discounts the cash flows for each sub-period at an interest rate (the internal rate of return) that makes the sum of the present values of the cash flows and value of the portfolio at the end equal to the portfolio value at the beginning of the period. The money-weighted return may be calculated as follows:

$$V_{beginning} = \frac{C1}{(1 + v)} + \frac{C2}{(1 + v)^2} + \ldots + \frac{Cn + V_{end}}{(1 + v)^n}$$

where:

V_{end} = the portfolio value at the end of the period
$V_{beginning}$ = the portfolio value at the beginning of the period
v = the money weighted rate of return.
Cn = the cash flow in period n.

For example, calculate the internal rate of return/money-weighted return when $V_{beginning}$ is £4.4 m and V_{end} is £4.5 m, and three distributions of £500 000 are made at the end of years 1, 2 and 3.

$$V_{beginning} = \frac{C1}{(1 + v)} + \frac{C2}{(1 + v)^2} + \ldots + \frac{Cn + V_{end}}{(1 + v)^n}$$

$$£4.4\,m = \frac{£0.5}{(1 + v)} + \frac{£0.5}{(1 + v)^2} + \frac{£0.5 + £4.5}{(1 + v)^3}$$

The money-weighted rate of return v can be shown to be 12% by either (i) choosing several different values, selecting the one that gives the answer nearest to £4.4 m and repeating this in an iterative process until the right answer is found; or (ii) selecting two values, one which gives a $V_{beginning}$ of more than £4.4 m and the other less than £4.4 m and extrapolating between the two.

Sometimes, the money-weighted method can give unexpected results. Performance can appear to be better than it actually is if money is invested in a fund during a period when the fund is performing well, say, after a period of performing poorly. The performance will be biased towards that time period when the cash invested was at its peak. A more accurate measure is the time-weighted return, which is not as affected by cash inflows into and cash outflows from the fund over which the portfolio manager has no control.

Time-weighted returns

The time-weighted return measures the compound growth rate of the value of the portfolio between any cash flow dates. It can be calculated as follows:

$$V_{portfolio} = [(1+v_1)(1+v_2) \ldots (1+v_n)] - 1$$

where:

n = the number of sub-periods
v_n = the return achieved in sub-period n.

When calculating the returns between each cash flow, the following method is used:

$$V_1 = \frac{D + V_e - V_s \times 100}{V_s}$$

where:

V_s = fund value just after the cash flow that established the start of the sub-period (or start of the period if at the beginning)

V_e = fund value just before the cash flow that established the end of the sub-period (or end of the period if at the end)

D = any returns paid out from the fund at the end of the holding period.

For example, a fund starts the year with a value of £40 million. It falls to £20 million by the middle of the year, when a further £20 million is invested bringing the fund back up to £40 million in total. The fund then rises to £80 million by year-end. To calculate the money-weighted return, for the first sub-period, the calculation is:

$$V1 = \frac{0 + £20 - £40}{£40} \times 100 = -50\%$$

The value at the start of the second sub-period is now £40 after £20 million was deposited, making the start of the sub-period. The fund then rises to £80 and the calculation is:

$$V2 = \frac{0 + £80 - £40}{£40} \times 100 = 100\%$$

Combining the two sub-periods results in the following:

$$V_{portfolio} = [(1+v_1)(1+v_2) \ldots (1+v_n)] - 1$$

$$= [(1 - 0.5) \times (1 + 1)] - 1$$

$$= 0$$

The overall period return is zero. The returns are basically combined as if they were compound interest in each sub-period to generate the time-weighted returns.

Usually, the money-weighted return delivers a greater value than the time-weighted return and is influenced by the cash coming in and out of the fund to a higher degree than is the time-weighted return. The time-weighted rate of return is often the preferred measure for calculating the return on a portfolio.

Performance evaluation

Clients, trustees and other interested parties will be interested not only in the absolute returns achieved by fund managers, but also in the returns achieved relative to returns attained by market indices or by other fund managers. To evaluate the performance of a fund manager, the investor usually specifies a relevant benchmark portfolio against which the manager's performance is measured. This can be a stock market index from one of the FTSE ranges, such as the FTSE-100 Index (100 largest companies by market capitalization), FT-Actuaries All Share Index or FTSE Small Cap Index. In actuality, any index can be used as a benchmark.

Alternatively the investor may use a peer group benchmark, where the fund's performance is measured against that of similar funds. In the UK, companies such as Combined Actuarial Performance Limited (CAPS), Micropal, Morningstar Europe and World Markets Company (WM) specialize in performance measurement, offering databases and indices that facilitate measuring the performance of pension funds, life funds, unit trusts and investment trusts by using peer group benchmarks. The CAPS median and WM benchmarks are most frequently used in measuring the performance of pension funds. Micropal and Morningstar Europe mainly specialize in the performance measurement of funds offered to the retail investor.

Beating an index consistently over time is a particularly difficult task for a portfolio manager to accomplish – in a perfect market this is considered practically impossible. Funds have transaction costs and expenses, which also have to be beaten. Many good managers are still likely to underperform periodically while those that out-perform the index consistently over time will only do so by relatively small percentages. As a matter of presentation, fund managers normally prefer peer group comparisons, which effectively eliminate some of the variables and show the fund manager's relative ranking against the competition.

Performance attribution

Performance of a fund can be further broken down into asset allocation decisions and stock selection. After assessing a fund manager's performance over time, it will become clear whether that fund manager is better at selecting asset classes or at picking winning stocks. The process of segregating the performance associated with asset allocation from that of stock selection is called performance attribution.

To work out the performance attribution, first a benchmark portfolio is constructed. Then a second, artificial benchmark portfolio is built, which has an initial asset mix equal to that of the original portfolio, and where cash flows are distributed by the same amounts between asset classes as in the fund manager's actual portfolio. What will differ are the returns given by the two benchmarks and by the actual portfolio, and these differences can be used to identify asset allocation attribution.

To illustrate this method of attribution analysis, consider an equity fund that contains both UK and US equities (assume that the exchange rate is fixed for the period of the analysis). At the beginning of the evaluation period, the fund is worth V_0 with x% invested in UK equities and y% invested in US equities. A benchmark portfolio is selected with the same UK–US equity proportions. The equity indices chosen to represent the benchmarks are the FTSE 100 and the S&P 500 indices. There is a cash inflow into the fund (C) halfway through the evaluation period. The fund manager makes a decision to invest z% of this payment into UK equities and the rest $(1 - z\%)$ into US equities. The fund manager has deviated from the original benchmark proportions. Given the following:

B_1 = total value of the benchmark portfolio at the end of the evaluation period

$B_{1,UK}$ = value of UK portion of the benchmark portfolio at end of the period

$B_{1,US}$ = value of US portion of the benchmark portfolio at end of the period

V_1 = the market value of the fund at the end of the evaluation period

C = cash inflow

r_1 = UK equity index return attained in first half of year

r_2 = UK equity index return attained in second half of year

r_3 = US equity index return attained in first half of year

r_4 = US equity index return attained in second half of year, the value of the actual benchmark portfolio, B_1, is:

$$B_1 = B_{1,UK} + B_{1,US}$$
$$B_{1,UK} = x\% \, V_0(1 + r_1)(1 + r_2) + x\%C(1 + r_2)$$
$$B_{1,US} = y\% \, V_0(1 + r_3)(1 + r_4) + y\%C(1 + r_4).$$

The value of the second, artificial benchmark fund B_2 is:

$$B_2 = B_{2,UK} + B_{2,US}$$
$$B_{2,UK} = x\% \, V_0(1 + r_1)(1+r_2) + z\%C(1 + r_2)$$
$$B_{2,US} = y\% \, V_0(1 + r_3)(1 + r_4) + (1 - z)\%C(1 + r_4)$$

The difference between the performance of the fund manager's portfolio and the benchmark is designated as:

$$V_1 - B_1$$

The difference between the benchmark and the artificial benchmark fund which is attributed to the difference in asset allocation is:

$$B_2 - B_1$$

These benchmarks differ only in respect to the allocation of the cash inflow into the fund. The difference between the benchmark fund and the artificial benchmark fund that is ascribed to asset selection is measured as:

$$V_1 - B_2$$

With these two funds, the portions invested in US and UK equities are equal and any difference will be due to the make-up of the portfolio manager's fund. Thus, the total performance of the portfolio can be given as follows:

$$\text{Total performance} = V_1 - B_1$$
$$= (V_1 - B_2) + (B_2 - B_1)$$

For example, A pension fund is composed of US equities and UK equities worth £500 million at the beginning of the year. The benchmark portfolio is designated to be 70% US (Dow Jones) and 30% UK (FTSE 100). At the beginning of the year the portfolio had the same asset allocation as the designated benchmark. Exactly at mid-year, though, the fund manager decided to rearrange the portions so that she held equal amounts of US and UK equities for the remainder of the year. In the first half of the year the US index rose 5% and the UK index rose 7%, and in the second half of the year the US index rose 9% and the UK index rose 4%. The portfolio's value at the end of the year is £569 million.

First, the value of the benchmark portfolio is calculated as follows:

$$B_1 = [0.70 \times £500 \times (1.05)(1.09)] + [0.30 \times £500(1.07)(1.04)]$$

$$= £567\,495\,000$$

The fund manager's performance versus the benchmark is:

$$V_1 - B_1 = £569\,000\,000 - £567\,495\,000$$

$$= £1\,505\,000$$

Second, the part of this performance that resulted from an asset allocation decision is determined by calculating the end of year value of the second benchmark portfolio:

$$\text{Value of } B_2 \text{ (after first half of year)} = [0.70 \times £500 \times (1.05)]$$

$$+ [0.30 \times £500 \times (1.07)]$$

$$= £528\,000\,000$$

$$\text{Value of } B_2 \text{ (after second half of year)} = [0.50 \times £528 \times (1.09)]$$

$$+ [0.50 \times £528 \times (1.04)]$$

$$= £562\,320\,000$$

$$B_2 - B_1 = £562\,320\,000 - £567\,495\,000$$

$$= -£5\,175\,000$$

$$V_1 - B_2 = £569\,000\,000 - £562\,320\,000$$

$$= £6\,680\,000$$

The conclusion is that the asset allocation decisions caused a decline in the value of the portfolio compared to the benchmark indices. However, the portfolio outperformed the main benchmark (B_1) as a result of good stock selection tactics. In this case, the fund manager has demonstrated poor asset allocation skills but good stock selection capabilities. The portfolio manager's performance would have to be monitored over time, even over several years, to determine whether she consistently delivered better stock selection results compared to asset allocation performance.

Risk-adjusted portfolio performance measures

Measuring the risk associated with a portfolio is one important aspect of measuring portfolio performance. Portfolio returns must be adjusted for risk before they can be compared meaningfully. The easiest way to adjust returns for portfolio risk is to compare rates of return amongst portfolios with similar risk profiles. This process may be misleading, however, for some managers may concentrate on particular subgroups, so that the portfolio profiles are not actually that comparable. More accurate measures of portfolio returns have come into vogue to calculate risk-adjusted returns using mean-variance criteria and measuring both risk and return. Risk-adjusted returns are not necessarily perfect measurements, as they do not take into account transaction costs. They are, however, important tools for providing information about portfolios. Three of the most popular risk-adjusted measures will now be examined. They differ from one another according to the risk measure used.

The Sharpe measure

The Sharpe ratio measures excess return per unit of risk, or, in other words, uses an estimate of total risk of a portfolio to calculate excess return to volatility (volatility being the standard deviation of the returns).

$$\text{Sharpe measure} = \frac{R_p - R_f}{\sigma_p}$$

where:

R_p = the return achieved on the portfolio
R_f = the return available from a risk-free asset
σ_p = the standard deviation of the return on the portfolio.

The higher the value of this measure the better value the portfolio represents, since as σ_p gets smaller the total risk of the portfolio gets smaller. If the Sharpe ratio is negative the portfolio's performance is less than the risk-free rate and the negative figure itself cannot be compared to other negative figures.

The Treynor measure

The Treynor ratio uses the beta coefficient or the systematic risk of the portfolio as its measure of risk. It is a measure of the portfolio's excess return with respect to its beta.

$$\text{Treynor measure} = \frac{R_p - R_f}{\beta_p}$$

where:

R_p = the return achieved on the portfolio
R_f = the return from the risk-free asset
β_p = the CAPM beta of the portfolio.

The higher the value of the Treynor measure the better the value represented by the portfolio, since a higher beta represents higher systematic risk. The Treynor measure may be preferred by investors who are running highly diversified portfolios, as the measure does not consider unsystematic risk. A portfolio holding a large number of investments should see the unsystematic risk diversified away. The Sharpe measure, which considers total risk, may be preferred by investors with less diversified portfolios.

The Jensen measure

The Jensen ratio calculates the excess return that a portfolio generates over that predicted by CAPM based on the beta of the portfolio and the average market return. Jensen's measure is the portfolio's alpha value. CAPM can be used to construct a benchmark portfolio with a given amount of systematic risk and measure the difference in return of this portfolio (benchmark) and the return achieved by the portfolio manager.

Jensen measure $= \alpha = R_p - R_b$

$R_b = R_f + \beta_b (R_m - R_f)$

where:

R_p = the return on the portfolio being evaluated
R_b = the return on the benchmark portfolio
β_b = the benchmark portfolio's CAPM beta.

To summarize:

- The Sharpe ratio looks at total risk
- The Treynor ratio takes into account systematic risk
- The Jensen measure looks at the performance of the portfolio over and above that of a benchmark.

If an investor has limited holdings, then standard deviation may provide a more accurate measure of risk. Likewise, if an investor holds a wide variety of holdings outside of one particular mutual fund, then beta may be a more accurate measure of risk.

For example, two fund managers are employed to manage two portfolios with identical objectives. Details of their portfolios are as follow:

Fund	*Return*	*Beta (β_p)*	*Total risk (σ_p)*
A	10%	1.03	10%
B	14%	1.25	20%

Using the Sharpe measure, where:

$$\text{Sharpe measure} = \frac{R_p - R_f}{\sigma_p} \quad (\text{assume } R_f = 4.5\%)$$

$$\text{Fund A} = \frac{10 - 4.5}{10} = 0.55$$

$$\text{Fund B} = \frac{14 - 4.5}{20} = 0.48$$

it can be concluded that, on a risk-adjusted basis considering total risk, fund manager A has outperformed fund manager B.

Using the Treynor measure, where:

$$\text{Treynor measure} = \frac{R_p - R_f}{\beta_p}$$

$$\text{Fund A} = \frac{10 - 4.5}{1.03} = 5.34\%$$

$$\text{Fund B} = \frac{14 - 4.5}{1.25} = 7.6\%$$

it can be concluded that, on a risk-adjusted basis taking into account systematic risk, fund manager B has outperformed fund manager A.

Using the Jensen measure, where:

$$\text{Jensen measure} = \alpha = R_p - R_b$$

$$R_b = R_f + \beta_b (R_m - R_f) \text{ (assume } R_m = 8\%)$$

$$R_a = 4.5 + 1.03(8 - 4.5) = 8.1\%$$
$$R_b = 4.5 + 1.25(8 - 4.5) = 8.9\%$$

$$\alpha_a = R_a = 10.0 - 8.1 = 1.9\%$$
$$\alpha_b = R_b = 14.0 - 8.9 = 5.1\%$$

it can be concluded that on a risk-adjusted basis (systematic risk), fund manager B has performed better than fund manager A.

One more point to note is that returns will be affected by tax rates, inflation over time, and foreign exchange rates when applicable.

Other measures

A couple of other measures of performance and risk that may sometimes be utilized are described below.

Tracking error

Similar to the Jensen measure, the tracking error relies on a benchmark or index and is defined as the standard deviation of the excess returns of the portfolio P relative to benchmark B. The tracking error is interpreted as a measure of how large the deviations between the portfolio and the benchmark have been historically. A high value generally indicates a higher relative risk.

Information ratio

The information ratio is defined as the difference between the returns of the portfolio and the benchmark, divided by the tracking error. A positive information ratio implies that the decision to deviate from the benchmark resulted in a higher return. The higher the historic information ratio, the more excess return (alpha) was obtained by the same risk taken (in terms of tracking error). Negative information ratios lead to the same problem as do negative Sharpe ratios, and hence are not usually reported.

Decomposing risk-adjusted returns

Once the alpha has been assessed (say from the example above using the Jensen measure), the next step is to identify the source of that performance. It might be assumed that the outperformance may have been due to the skill of the portfolio manager in selecting stocks. However, in selecting these stocks the manager may have taken greater specific risk into the portfolio. (The Jensen measure may be inappropriate as a risk-adjusted measure of portfolio performance if the portfolio includes a lot of specific risk.)

The Fama decomposition of total return helps to separate into components the total return in the case where the relevant measure of risk is systematic risk or beta (see Figure 3.1).

The total return R_p can be decomposed into four components:

Return on the portfolio = Risk-free rate
+ Return from the client's risk parameters
+ Return from market timing
+ Return from security selection

The first component of the return on the portfolio is the **risk-free rate**. Fund managers are expected to earn, at the very least, the risk-free rate.

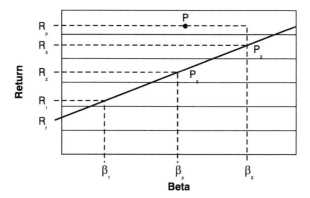

Figure 3.1 Analysis of total return

Usually, clients expect a degree of return above the risk-free rate. The client's tolerance for risk can be measured by β_1, for example, and the client will expect a return on the portfolio of at least R_1. The return from the **client's risk profile** is thus $(R_1 - R_f)$.

The return from the **market timing** can also be known as the return from the fund manager's risk. That is because the portfolio manager will often choose a portfolio with a beta that differs from the beta expected by the client. When the portfolio manager has an implicitly more bullish view than the client, the manager will decide to raise the beta of the portfolio above the client's risk-tolerance beta, and will invest a larger proportion of the funds in a market portfolio and a lesser portion in the risk-free asset than the client would have selected. With a portfolio beta of β_p, the expected return is R_2 and the market timing can be calculated as $(R_2 - R_1)$.

One caveat regarding market timing and risk-adjusted measures in general is that they only take into account the average risk of the portfolio. The risks and betas of a portfolio may vary on an extreme basis over the course of an evaluation period. Therefore, the average risk measure calculated may be misleading. If the portfolio manager changes the risk profile extensively to attempt to time stock purchases and sales, calculating the average risk taken will not accurately measure whether, on a risk-adjusted basis, the manager has been successful in timing the purchases and the sales. One way around this problem is to assess the performance of the fund manager on a rolling basis. For instance, if the return on the relevant market consistently rises just after the fund manager has increased the portfolio's beta, it could be said that the fund manager was able to demonstrate good judgment in terms of market timing.

The next component of total return is **security selection**, or $(R_p - R_2)$, and is also known as the return to selectivity. Considering portfolios P and P_2, they both have the same amount of market risk given that they have the same beta, β_p. They do, however, have different total risks. Since portfolio P_2 lies on the security market line, it contains no undiversifiable risk. Portfolio P, though, lies above the SML, and is not a linear combination of the market portfolio and the risk-free asset. Portfolios that lie on the SML derived from the CAPM are considered to be linear combinations of the market portfolio and the risk-free rate. It can be concluded that portfolio P differs from portfolio P_2 because P's portfolio manager has engaged in active security selection. Portfolio P has delivered additional returns, but the fund manager has had to increase diversifiable risk to do so.

Since R_p is greater than R_3 in this example, the conclusion is that the risk taken in selecting the stocks in P was successful. The extra return from taking on additional diversifiable risk is $(R_3 - R_2)$, but the additional return $(R_p - R_3)$ is due to pure selectivity.

For example, if the total return of a portfolio (R_p) is 10%, calculate the decomposition of returns, given portfolio and market data as follows:

R_p = 10%
R_m = 8%
σ_p = 7%
σ_m = 6%
β_p = 0.9
r_f = 5%
β_{Client} = 0.8

Return from client's risk

As the client designates a beta of 0.8 as the preferred beta, the return from the client's desired portfolio is:

$R_1 = 5 + 0.8 (8 - 5)$

$\quad = 7.4\%$

The interpretation here is that the return from the client's risk is:

$(R_1 - R_f) = 7.4\% - 5\%$

$\qquad\quad = 2.4\%$

Return from market timing

The beta of the portfolio is actually 0.9. Subsequently, the expected return on the actual portfolio is thus:

$R_2 = 5 + 0.9 (8 - 5)$

$\quad = 7.7\%$

and this provides the return from market timing as:

$(R_2 - R_1) = 7.7\% - 7.4\%$

$\qquad\quad = 0.3\%$

This return is due to the decision by the fund manager to take a risk (fund manager risk) because he or she is bullish about the market. The beta that the fund manager chooses is higher than the one expected by the client.

Return from selectivity

As the final return of the portfolio was 10%, the return based on selectivity can be derived as:

$(R_p - R_2) = 10\% - 7.7\%$

$\qquad\quad = 2.3\%$

The fund performed better than expected for the given beta, and this is due to stock selection.

The return from selectivity can be sub-analysed into return from diversifiable risk and return from pure selectivity by the fund manager.

Return from diversifiable risk:

First, locate a portfolio P_3 with the same total risk as the given portfolio (P) with the 10%. This portfolio will have a beta as follows:

$$B_3 = \frac{\sigma_p}{\sigma_m}$$

$$= \frac{7\%}{6\%}$$

$$= 1.17$$

The expected return from this portfolio will be:

$$R_3 = 5\% + 1.17(8\% - 5\%)$$

$$= 8.51\%$$

As a result, the return from diversifiable risk is:

$$(R_3 - R_2) = 8.51\% - 7.7\%$$

$$= 0.81\%$$

Pure selectivity:

The final calculation is that of the return to pure selectivity and is as follows:

$$(R_p - R_3) = 10\% - 8.51\%$$

$$= 1.49\%$$

Summary

The total returns have been decomposed as summarized below:

Risk-free rate	5.0%		5.0%
		➤	2.4%
Return from client's beta	7.4%		
		➤	0.3%
Return from manager's beta	7.7%		
		➤	0.81%
Return from portfolio σ	8.51%		
		➤	1.49%
Total return	10.0%		10.0%

In other words, the return to market risk is 2.7% while the return to selectivity is 2.3%. Adding these to the risk-free rate of 5%, the total return of 10% is attained.

Quiz: Chapter 3

1   What is the time-weighted return for the three-month evaluation period, given the following data?

Month 1   +5%
Month 2   +4%
Month 3   +3%

(A)   4.0%
(B)   12.0%
(C)   10.24%
(D)   12.48%
(E)   4.58%

2   The value of a portfolio at the beginning of a time period is £60 million and its value at the end of the time period is £70 million. Assuming a £5 million cash inflow was paid into the fund at the beginning of the period, what is the money return?

A)   16.7%
(B)   10.5%
(C)   8.3%
(D)   25.0%
(E)   5.8%

3   Measuring the returns of a portfolio versus the returns of other portfolios with similar risk mandates is known as:

(A)   Money-weighted return
(B)   Attribution analysis
(C)   Geometric index evaluation
(D)   Time-weighted return
(E)   Peer group comparison

4 _____ is the internal rate of return of the fund opening and closing values along with any deposits into or withdrawals out of the fund.

(A) Time-weighted return
(B) Money-weighted return
(C) Money return
(D) Attribution analysis
(E) Peer group comparison

5 Assume a fund consists of US equities and Japanese equities worth $100 million at the beginning of the year. The portfolio to which the fund is benchmarked is comprised of 60% US equities (S & P 500) and 40% Japanese equities (Nikkei 225). At the beginning of the year the fund had the same asset allocation as the designated benchmark. Halfway through the year, however, the fund manager decided to change the weightings so that the fund now held 40% US equities and 60% Japanese equities for the remainder of the year. In the first half of the year the US index fell 2% and the Japanese index rose 5%, and in the second half of the year the US index rose 3% and the Japanese index rose 1%. The fund's value at the end of the year is $125 million. What portion of the return is attributable to asset allocation, and what portion is attributable to stock selection?

(A) –$369 600; $1 386 600
(B) –$369 600; $1 016 000
(C) $1 386 600; –$369 600
(D) $416 000; $4 000 000
(E) $–369 600; $1 016 000

6 If two funds present the following:

Fund	Return	β	Total Risk
A	18%	1.2	17%
B	12%	1.05	15%

Using the Sharpe measure, which fund manager outperforms?
Using the Treynor measure, which fund manager outperforms?
(Assume the risk-free rate = 4.5%).

(A)   Sharpe measure,   A outperforms;
      Treynor measure, A outperforms
(B)   Sharpe measure,   B outperforms;
      Treynor measure, B outperforms
(C)   Sharpe measure,   A outperforms;
      Treynor measure, B outperforms
(D)   Sharpe measure,   B outperforms;
      Treynor measure, A outperforms
(E)   Sharpe measure,   both equal;
      Treynor measure, both equal

7   Given the data below, what is the return from selectivity?

R_p = 6%
R_m = 5%
σ_p = 5%
σ_m = 6%
β_p = 1.1
r_f = 4.5%
β_{Client} = 0.7

(A)   0.35%
(B)   0.20%
(C)   1.10%
(D)   0.70%
(E)   0.95%

Chapter 4

Indices

Indices are widely used to monitor the current level of a market and to measure historical rates of return. A securities index gauges the performance of a certain basket of securities. For example, the Dow Jones Industrial Average (DJIA) is an index of the stock prices of 30 large companies representative of American industry. There are numerous other indices utilized in the securities markets, and new ones are constantly being developed.

Importance of indices

Indices are significant for several reasons. In actuality, they provide a general measure of the performance of the economy. For example, it is uncommon for a stock market to be consistently rising during a period of economic downturn. Also, as mentioned previously, indices are often used to evaluate the performance of the funds that fund managers are running. Similarly, some funds attempt to replicate indices and deliver the same returns as the indices that they mimic. Analysts use indices to assess the overall direction of markets, and indices are used to estimate statistical parameters such as beta. Additionally, indices can be utilized as the basis for various derivative securities.

The effectiveness of an index depends on the following factors:

1 The market covered
2 The types of securities included in the index
3 How many securities are included
4 How the index is calculated
5 How the index is adjusted over time for changes in securities (such as takeovers).

Some of these factors are relatively straightforward. Some indices focus on specific industries or sectors, whilst others focus on markets or countries. Also, some indices have a small number of stocks, and others have a huge number – such as the Wilshire 5000 Total Market index in the US, which is comprised of over 5000 companies. How indices are calculated and adjusted over time is not necessarily clear-cut. Several methods exist to construct indices.

It is therefore important to understand the different methodologies used for calculating indices. Here, simple arithmetic indices, geometric indices and market-value-weighted indices are examined. Depending on the type of fund management strategy employed, periodic index rebalancing may affect portfolio investment decisions. For example, portfolios that track indices directly will buy or sell securities on the day that the index changes to match the new components and weights of the rebalanced index. Portfolios that take on more risk compared to the benchmark may try to estimate the rebalancing effects ahead of the rebalancing date and adjust their portfolios accordingly in order to gain extra performance.

Overall, portfolio managers and other investors can monitor the level of a market using an index, and can use this information to time investment decisions. Specialized indices can be created to monitor the performance of funds that are measured against indices that are not already quoted.

The concept of price relative solidifies the basis of how indices are calculated. The price of any share can be monitored by comparing its price at time t (P_t) with its price at some earlier base date (P_0). Thus, P_t/P_0 is called the price relative calculation (P_0 must be adjusted for capital changes like scrip or rights issues). Indices look at the relative price changes of a series of constituents over time.

The percentage change relative to the base date can be calculated as follows:

$$\text{Percentage change} = \frac{Pt - P0}{P0}$$

Whilst the calculation for percentage points movement between two points in time is simply:

$$\text{Percentage points movement} = Pt - P0$$

These two measures should not be confused, as they are quite different.

Indices can be categorized as either price-weighted or value-weighted. With a price-weighted index, securities are held in the index in proportion to their prices. With a value-weighted index, securities are held in proportion to their total company market values.

Price-weighted indices

Sometimes, price-weighted indices are considered to be equally weighted as the index assigns the same weighting to each constituent. Each stock is designed to have equal influence on the index.

Arithmetic indices

A simple arithmetic index is calculated to indicate the average price of a series of shares by starting with a base value of 100 (although other base values can be chosen) and then adding together the prices of all the relevant constituents of the series before dividing them by the sum of the prices of the constituents at the base date:

$$\text{Arithmetic index} = \text{Base index value} \times \frac{\text{Sum of current values}}{\text{Sum of base values}}$$

Consider the following example of the calculation of a simple arithmetic index for stocks A and B:

Time period	Share price A	Share price B	Value of Index
0	100	100	100.0
1	113	90	101.5
2	120	85	102.5
3	110	60	85.0
4	90	0	45.0

The index value at time $0 = 100 \times (100 + 100)/(100 + 100) = 100$

The index value at time $2 = 100 \times (120 + 85)/(100 + 100) = 102.5$

When the share price of B goes to 0 at time 4, the value of the index is worth half of the value of Share A.

An arithmetic index is the most appropriate alternative for portfolio performance measurement, as the returns on a portfolio will be the sum of the returns of the individual shares within the portfolio. Examples of simple aggregate price indices include the Dow Jones Industrial Average and the Nikkei Stock Average.

Re-basing indices

Occasionally, indices are re-based or set to a new base value. To do this, the following formula is used:

$$\text{Value of re-based index} = 100 \times \frac{\text{Value of the index at time t}}{\text{Value of the index at the time it is to be re-based}}$$

If re-basing the series used in the previous example, to set the index equal to 100 at time 2 it would be necessary to divide each index observation by 102.5 and multiply these values by 100:

Time period	Index
0	$(100.0/102.5) \times 100 = 97.56$
1	$(101.5/102.5) \times 100 = 99.02$
2	$(102.5/102.5) \times 100 = 100.0$
3	$(85.0/102.5) \times 100 = 82.93$
4	$(45.0/102.5) \times 100 = 43.90$

Other considerations

With simple arithmetic indices, the effects of stock splits, dividends and other changes affecting stocks over time must be considered. For example, in a two for one share split, all current shareholders will receive two new shares for each old share they own in the company. The total value of the company has not changed, but there are twice as many shares, each worth twice as much. Since the price of the stock falls, the price-weighted index falls even though nothing has really changed in an economic sense. For a price-weighted index, this problem can be dealt with by adjusting the divisor each time a split occurs. Changing the divisor adjusts the index for these artificial changes so that the index continues to reflect the actual value of the underlying securities. As mentioned, the Dow Jones Industrial Average is a price-weighted average of 30 US industrial stocks. Originally the divisor was 30, though over time the divisor has been adjusted for stock splits and dividends and is now just a small fraction.

One advantage of the price-weighted index is that it is relatively simple to copy the rate of return of the index by buying the same number of shares of each stock in the index. This is useful for funds that are attempting to deliver returns similar to the index. However, there is no good reason for the index to be biased towards stocks which are higher in price as prices can be manipulated via stock splits. A high-priced stock will suddenly become less influential after its split and resulting decline in price. Thus, the value-weighted indices were developed to address this type of setback. However, a problem that can occur with both types of indices is **index staleness**, which results when stocks do not trade every day. If stocks in an index have not traded recently, the index will not necessarily reflect all current price information. Index staleness can occur primarily in indices that comprise a large number of securities, or in those indices that include more obscure or smaller capitalized stocks.

Geometric indices

Another method of creating an index from price relative values is the geometric index. This index is created as follows:

$$\text{Geometric index} = \text{Base index value} \times \sqrt[n]{\frac{\text{Product of current values}}{\text{Product of base values}}}$$

To continue with the previous example, a geometric index is calculated based on the price changes for shares A and B over four time periods:

Time period	Share price A	Share price B	Value of Index Arithmetic	Geometric
0	100	100	100.0	100.00
1	113	90	101.5	100.85
2	120	85	102.5	101.00
3	110	60	85.0	81.24
4	90	0	45.0	0.0

$$\text{Thus, the geometric index value at time 1} = 100 \times \sqrt{\frac{(113 \times 90)}{(100 \times 100)}}$$

$$= 100.85.$$

Unlike the simple arithmetic index, the geometric index does not reflect the value of an equally weighted portfolio of stocks. For example, when the price of share B falls to 0, the value of the geometric index becomes 0.

There are some further pitfalls in using geometric indices:

1 This type of index tends to understate the performance relative to an equivalently weighted arithmetic index because it is less sensitive to large price increases and more sensitive to large price falls
2 A geometric index is not likely to be representative of achievable performance as the return on a portfolio is the sum of the constituents, not the product thus using it as a benchmark would not be prudent. Its value would always be less than, or equal to, the value of an equally weighted portfolio of its constituents.

The Financial Times Ordinary Share Index (FT30 Share Index) is an example of an equally weighted, geometric index. This index is based on 30 large stocks that are quoted on the London Stock Exchange and are supposed to reflect the nature of the UK economy.

Market-value-weighted indices

Equally weighted indices do not necessarily accurately reflect the changes in the value of a market as the value of its constituents change. Equally weighted indices end up giving too much weight to the price changes of assets with low market capitalization, and too little weight to the price changes of assets with larger market capitalization (relatively speaking). For example, a 1% change in the price of a very small firm is given the same weight as a 1% change in the price of a very large firm. To overcome these problems, market-value-weighted arithmetic price indices are calculated.

Issues to be considered regarding the weighting quantity to be used include:

■ Weighting by the original quantity for both original and current prices
■ Weighting by the current quantity for both original and current prices
■ Weighting by the original quantity for original prices and current quantity for current prices
■ Weighting equally (i.e. the average price relative index).

Regarding arithmetic index calculations, all versions are used for different purposes. In relation to geometric means, however, the third method is the only one that needs to be considered.

If the concept of weightings or quantities is introduced, this provides a more accurate method of determining the relative importance of items within a series. The question remains, however, should the base year or current year quantities or weights be used? Either can be used, but it is important that the same weights be used throughout the calculations. Both produce different kinds of index numbers with respective advantages and disadvantages.

Laspeyre index

The Laspeyre index is a base-period quantity-weighted index (all prices are weighted by the base-date quantities). The calculation for this index is:

$$\text{Laspeyre Index} = \frac{\Sigma P_n Q_0}{\Sigma P_0 Q_0} \times \text{Base index value}$$

where:

P_n = current period price
Q_0 = weighting or quantity at base period
P_0 = base period price.

This index indicates how much the cost of buying base-period quantities at current prices is, compared with base-period costs. The following example illustrates the use of the Laspeyre index using data related to the calculation of food price inflation rates (assume a base index of 100).

Item	Base		Current	
	$P_0(£)$	Q_0	$P_n(£)$	Q_n
A	1.00	20	4.00	5
B	1.15	18	2.20	15
C	1.30	12	2.15	18
D	2.00	15	2.05	20

The Laspeyre index calculation is as follows:

Item	$P_n Q_0(£)$	$P_0 Q_0(£)$
A	80.00	20.00
B	39.60	20.70
C	25.80	15.60
D	30.80	30.00
	176.2	86.30

$$\frac{176.20}{86.30} \times 100 = 204.17$$

This index measures how the original shopping basket has changed in price. If this index were applied to a portfolio calculation, it would show how the original portfolio has changed in value.

Paasche index

A Paasche price index is a current-period quantity-weighted index (all prices are weighted by the current quantities). The calculation for this index is:

$$\text{Paasche index} = \frac{\Sigma P_n Q_n}{\Sigma P_0 Q_n} \times \text{Base index value}$$

where:

P_n = current period price
Q_n = weighting or quantity at current
P_0 = base period price.

This type of index measures how current-period costs are related to the cost of buying current-period quantities. Thus, using the data from the example of above one can calculate the Paasche Index:

Item	$P_n Q_n$ £	$P_0 Q_n$ £
A	20.00	8.00
B	33.00	17.25
C	38.70	23.40
D	41.00	40.00
	132.70	88.65

$$\frac{132.7}{88.65} \times 100 = 149.70$$

This index measures how the current shopping basket has changed in price. If looking at a portfolio, it would measure how the current portfolio has changed in value.

Comparison of the Laspeyre and Paasche indices

Although either index can be used, there are advantages and disadvantages attached to each.

The advantages of the Laspeyre index include the following:

■ The weights are taken from base-period figures, and thus new prices will be the only data to be collected each time a new index is to be produced.

The Paasche index requires new prices and weights each time, so more data must be collected.

■ The Laspeyre index requires less recalculation each time because the denominator remains constant.

■ Because the denominator remains constant for the Laspeyre index, it is easier to make comparisons year to year. A Paasche index can only be compared with the base year because the weights change for every index.

The advantages of the Paasche index include:

■ The Paasche index is believed to give a truer result in terms of current consumer patterns because it uses the current period weightings. In addition, there may be occasions when quantities or weights vary to such a high degree from year to year that it would be unrealistic to use a base-year quantity over a number of years, as with the Laspeyre index.

According to one source, Laspeyre indices are more common than Paasche indices. However, as the Laspeyre index is based on the original quantities or weights and does not take into account any switch into items that are

Table 4.1 Major stock indices

Index	Market	Number of shares	Type of index*
FT Ordinary Share	UK	30	GU
FTSE 100	UK	100	AW
FTSE Mid-250	UK	250	AW
FTSE 350 Actuaries	UK	350	AW
FTSE Small Cap	UK		AW
FTSE Actuaries All Share	UK		AW
FTSE Eurotop 100	Europe	100	AW
FTSE Eurotop 300	Europe	300	AW
Dow Jones Industrial Average	USA	30	AU
Standard and Poors 500	USA	500	AW
Nikkei 225	Japan	225	AU

*A, arithmetic; G, geometric; U, unweighted; W, weighted.

rising quickly, this index may understate portfolio performance. On the other hand, the Paasche index may overstate portfolio performance, as its weighting is biased towards the items showing the smallest price increases.

The FT All Share index is an example of a market-value-weighted index.

Major stock indices

Table 4.1 summarizes how the main international stock indices are calculated.

Quiz: Chapter 4

1 What is the value of the simple arithmetic index after time 3, given the following data:

Time period	Share price A	Share price B
0	100	100
1	90	105
2	85	120
3	70	125

(A) 102.5
(B) 96.5
(C) 101.5
(D) 97.5
(E) 100.0

2 Using the above data, what is the value of the geometric index after time 2?

(A) 100.00
(B) 93.54
(C) 96.82
(D) 97.21
(E) 101.00

3 _____ can occur when stocks within an index do not trade every day, resulting in possible distortions of the true value of some of the components within the index.

(A) Index staleness
(B) Index divisor adjustment
(C) Index re-basing
(D) Index recalculation
(E) Index reweighting

4 Given the following details for two typical years of cost per product for products in category X (assume the base index value is 100), what is the value of the Paasche price index?

Item	Base year		Current year	
	$P_0(\text{£})$	Q_0	$P_n(\text{£})$	Q_n
A	4.00	20	4.25	25
B	5.15	34	5.10	36
C	6.20	55	6.35	60
D	6.85	16	6.99	20

(A) 101.95
(B) 102.05
(C) 101.55
(D) 102.34
(E) 103.10

5 Using the above data, what is the value of the Laspeyre price index?

(A) 101.95
(B) 102.05
(C) 101.55
(D) 102.34
(E) 103.10

6 What is one of the disadvantages of the Paasche index?

(A) The Paasche index overstates portfolio performance as its weighting is biased towards items showing the smallest price increase
(B) The Paasche index requires less recalculation because the denominator remains constant
(C) The Paasche index is believed to give a less true result in terms of consumer patterns because it uses base-period weightings
(D) The Paasche index requires fewer data to be collected
(E) The use of the Paasche index is likely to be more common than that of the Laspeyre index

Chapter 5

Bond portfolio management

Although most of this book is dedicated to equity portfolio management theory and practice, this chapter presents some of the issues surrounding bond portfolio management. First a few preliminaries on fixed income valuation are discussed, followed by some of the risk management techniques associated with bond portfolio management.

Bond calculations

First, some basic bond mathematics is reviewed.

Compound interest

Consider a situation in which a portfolio manager receives £9 000 000. He undertakes to repay the money seven years hence, with interest compounded at 14% semi-annually. Given that the interest is paid semi-annually, the effective annual rate of interest is $(1 + 0.07) \times (1 + 0.07) - 1 = 14.49\%$. The formula for calculating the amount due in seven years' time is:

$$S = P (1 + r)^n$$

where:

P = principal
S = sum at maturity
r = interest rate per year

n = time period in years.

The future commitment is therefore $S = £9\,000\,000 \times (1 + 0.1449)^7 = £23\,206\,807$ (subject to rounding error). This is summarized as:

Lump sum investment	£9 000 000
Semi annual interest	14%
Period of investment (in years)	7
Future commitment	£23 206 807

Bond yields

The value of an investment will depend on the return that it renders. For bonds, the single most important measure of return is the yield. There are several ways of calculating bond yields. The simplest measure used is the **current yield**. This measure assesses the cash return generated by an investment over the cash price or, simply, the return generated on money invested, assuming that prices remain constant.

$$\text{Current yield} = \frac{\text{Annual coupon}}{\text{Bond price}} \times 100$$

The coupon is the interest paid by the bond. For example, if the bond price is £100 and the coupon is £7, then the current yield is 7%. If the price goes up to £110, then the current yield falls to 6.36%. If the price of the bond falls to £90, then the current yield increases to 7.78%. Although the bond price changes, the coupon remains constant. However, the bond's current yield is inversely related to its price.

One flaw with the current yield calculation is that it ignores the time value of money. If an investor were offered the choice between receiving the £7 now or in two years' time, the choice would be to take the money now since it could then be invested to generate interest.

The yield to maturity resolves the issue of the time value of money. The bond's yield to maturity is, in effect, the discount rate that equates the bond's price with the computed present value of its cash flows (coupon payments and principal or redemption amount). It is the internal rate of return (IRR) generated by the cash flows of a bond. In general, the term 'yield' refers to the bond's yield to maturity or gross redemption yield. The formula is given below:

$$\text{Current bond price} = \frac{C_1}{(1 + y)} + \frac{C_2}{(1 + y)^2} + \frac{C_3}{(1 + y)^3} \cdots \frac{C_t + P}{(1 + y)^t}$$

where:

C_1 = coupon paid at the end of time period 1
C_t = coupon paid at the end of time period t (at maturity)
P = principal repaid at the end of time period t
y = yield to redemption or maturity.

There is no simple way of calculating the yield. Bond calculators and financial spreadsheets rely on a process of iteration, where the calculation is repeated with different values for y until the correct rate is found. Otherwise, numbers have to be plugged into the formula until the solution is achieved via trial and error.

Another method is to discount each flow by an appropriate interest rate for that time period and then to consider the present value of the flows against the current market price.

Annuity valuation

Assume that the portfolio manager from the example above decides to invest in a bond with the following specifications:

Bond maturity	17 years
Yield to maturity	14.49%
Price	100
Coupon	7% per coupon
Par value purchased	£9 000 000

In order to see how much money he will have in seven years (assuming interest rates stay at 14.49%), first calculate the future value of the coupons, and second the value of the bond at maturity. During the seven years the portfolio manager will receive fourteen coupons, each valued at 7% × £9 000 000 = £630 000. Assuming that this money is placed on deposit at 14.49% each time it is received, the amount to which it will accumulate in the future must be calculated. The following formula can be utilized:

$$AF = \frac{(1 + r)^n - 1}{r}$$

where:

AF = the future value of an annuity
r = the half-yearly interest rate
n = the number of coupons.

Using the given figures, the annuity factor becomes:

$$\frac{(1 + 0.07)^{14} - 1}{0.07} = 22.55$$

This means that if £630 000 is invested every six months for seven years, it will accumulate to £630 000 × 22.55 = £14 206 807 (subject to rounding).

Bond valuation

In seven years, the bond will have ten years to maturity. The portfolio manager will then sell the bond in order to meet the future commitment. To value this, treat the bond as two separate securities:

1 An annuity equivalent to the coupon payments for n half years
2 A zero coupon bond that pays par value at maturity.

The formula for the present value of an annuity factor is:

$$PAF = \frac{(1 - (1 + r)^{-n})}{r}$$

and for a zero coupon bond is:

$$Z = \frac{\text{Par value}}{(1 + r)^n}$$

The value of the bond in the above case with ten years to maturity is:

$$\text{PAF} = \frac{(1 - (1 + 0.07)^{-20})}{0.07} = 10.594$$

and for a zero coupon bond:

$$Z = \frac{£9\,000\,000}{(1 + 0.07)^{20}} = £2\,325\,771$$

The present value of the bond with ten years to maturity is therefore $10.594 \times 630\,000 + £2\,325\,771 = £9\,000\,000$. The total value is $£9\,000\,000 + £14\,206\,807 = £23\,206\,807$.

The above example is summarized as:

Bond maturity (in years)	17
Yield to maturity	14.49%
Coupon p.a.	14%
Par value purchased	£9 000 000.00
Value in 7 years	£23 206 807.35

It can be seen from the above that the portfolio manager exactly meets his target when interest rates are 14.49%, but may fail to meet his target when interest rates change. The formula assumes that the coupons received are reinvested at the same rate as the yield. If the portfolio manager is only going to be able to reinvest the coupons at a lower rate, then the overall return generated by the bond will be lower than the yield.

Duration

Duration (also known as Macaulay duration) is a measure of a bond's sensitivity to interest rate changes. However, the sensitivity of a bond to movements in the interest rate is influenced by a number of different factors. For instance, bonds with a longer dated maturity will be more sensitive to changes in the interest rate than bonds with a shorter maturity. With regard to the coupon, the lower coupon bonds demonstrate the greatest degree of sensitivity to the yield. The lower coupon bonds have more of their value linked to the terminal value. With a zero coupon bond which pays no coupons the entire value of the security is in the final payment, and if yields are high then the flows in the future are worth less and the sensitivity is diminished. It should be noted that the relationship between the coupon and maturity and the price is not symmetrical. This relationship is called convexity, and will be addressed below.

Thus duration is a composite measure of risk and is effectively the weighted average length of time to the receipt of a bond's payments (coupon and principal). Duration values are stated in years. The weight associated with each cash flow is proportional to the present value of each cash flow. The concept is designated Figure 5.1, where the triangle or point of balance represents the duration of the bond:

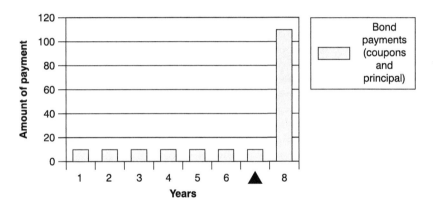

Figure 5.1   Duration

In a bond portfolio there will be a number of different bonds, each with a distinctive cash flow structure and yield. Each of these bonds will have a mathematical duration which shows how sensitive the bond is to interest rate changes. The relationship between bond prices and interest rate changes is illustrated in Figure 5.2.

As noted previously, bond prices have an inverse relationship with interest rates. This means that as interest rates go up bond prices go down, and vice versa. The straight line in Figure 5.2 indicates the duration estimate of the price change. The duration assumes that there is a linear relationship

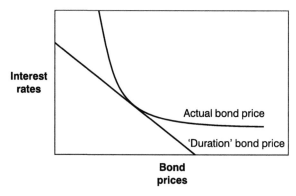

Figure 5.2 Duration and convexity

between interest rates and bond prices, while in reality there is a curved relationship. It means that the linear approximation will only be accurate if there are very small changes in the interest rate, and will be very inaccurate if the interest rates move by large amounts. The diagram also illustrates that when interest rates fall, bond prices will increase by an amount that is greater than that calculated by the duration. Conversely, when interest rates rise, the fall in the bond price will not be as great as that estimated by the duration. For this reason, bonds that have high convexity will be worth relatively more than bonds with low convexity when interest rates are very volatile. Convexity thus represents the curvature of the bond's price–yield curve, or the rate of change of the slope of the price–yield curve.

Calculating duration

To review, the present value of the future income flows generated by a bond is effectively what a buyer would be prepared to pay for the bond. This can be summarized in the formula:

$$B = \sum_{t=1}^{T} \frac{C_t}{(1 + y)^t}$$

where:

C_t = the value of each cash flow at time t
y = the yield of the bond.

Consider the example below. The procedure for calculating the value of a bond here is to take the present value of the future income flows. A bond has a yearly coupon of £12, and has ten years to run before it matures. There are therefore ten separate cash flows and, because they will be received in the future, they must be discounted to their present value. The yield is 5%.

	Coupon amount	*Discount using 5%*	*Present value*	*PV × No. of years*
1	12	0.9524	11.4286	11.4286
2	12	0.9070	10.8844	21.7687
3	12	0.8638	10.3661	31.0982
4	12	0.8227	9.8724	39.4897
5	12	0.7835	9.4023	47.0116
6	12	0.7462	8.9546	53.7275
7	12	0.7107	8.5282	59.6972
8	12	0.6768	8.1221	64.9766
9	12	0.6446	7.7353	69.6178
10	12	0.6139	68.7583	687.5828
Total			154.0521	1086.3986
Macaulay duration				7.0521
Modified duration				6.7163

The figure of 687.5828 is obtained by taking the present value of the cash flow for that year, 68.75, and multiplying it by t (which in this case is 10).

Since what is required is calculation of the duration, the total of the adjusted cash flows is divided by the price of the bond: 1086/154 = 7.05 years. This calculation is also called Macaulay duration.

Modified duration and convexity

Whilst Macaulay duration looks at the sensitivity of a bond to changes in the interest rate, modified duration evaluates the impact of yield changes on the price. Modified duration can be utilized to approximate the change in a bond's price, given a small change in the required yield.

The formula for modified duration is:

$$\text{Modified duration} = \frac{\text{Macauley duration}}{1 + y}$$

where y = the yield.

Finally, as the formula suggests, the figure 7.0521 is divided by (1 + y) in order to obtain the modified duration:

$$\text{Modified duration} = \frac{7.0521}{1.05} = 6.7163$$

If the yield (y) were to increase to 5.1%, given the modified duration formula it is possible to calculate the approximate change in the bond's price. Using the following formula, the change in bond's price given a change in the yield can be calculated:

Approximate change in bond price = (−Modified duration) × (Δy) × (B)

where:

Δy = change in yield

B = present value of the bond.

Using the example above, the calculation is:

Change in bond price = (−6.7163) × (0.001) × (£154.0521) = −£1.035

Therefore, if the yield increases from 5.0% to 5.1%, the price of the bond will fall by about £1.04.

As mentioned above, the relationship between yield and price is convex — that is, non-linear. Convexity will cause the modified duration to be overstated when the bonds fall in price, and understated when the bonds rise in price. However, when yield changes are small in value the modified duration calculation will provide a good estimate. There may only be problems if the change in yield is of a substantive value.

Portfolio duration

The portfolio duration is simply the weighted average of the individual durations of the bonds within the portfolio. Often risk managers set targets for their portfolio, and from time to time they may need to decrease the inherent interest rate risk associated with the portfolios. This will depend on the priorities of the investors.

Immunizing a portfolio

Immunization is a technique used by bond managers that allows them to meet a promised stream of cash outflows with a high degree of certainty. Immunization is achieved by calculating the duration of the promised outflow and then investing in a portfolio of bonds that has an identical duration. Provided the duration calculations are correct and there is no risk of a major convexity adjustment, the danger of not having sufficient cash to meet a future commitment is limited. The duration of a bond portfolio is simply calculated as the weighted average of the individual bonds within the portfolio.

As interest rates fluctuate, both the value of securities held in the portfolio and the rate at which those securities generate income fluctuates. Immunization, or the matching of assets on a duration basis, lets the portfolio meet its obligations despite interest rate movements. If yields rise, the portfolio's losses owing to the selling of a three-year bond in two years' time will be exactly offset by the gains from reinvesting the maturing one-year bond. Alternatively, if yields fall, the loss from being able to invest in a one-year bond will be exactly offset by being able to sell the three-year bond in two years at a premium. Therefore, the portfolio is immunized from the effect of any movement in interest rates.

Problems with immunization

One problem with immunization is that duration does not stay constant. With small changes in interest rates, duration will not change; however, when there is a significant change in interest rates, duration will change and the portfolio manager must therefore re-balance the portfolio with bonds of the new duration. The problem with this is that frequent re-balancing increases transactional costs and so the portfolio manager may have difficulty in achieving the re-balancing yield. Less frequent re-balancing will mean that the duration is allowed to change without sufficient attempts being made to track that change. The portfolio manager in these circumstances faces a trade-off.

Immunization strategies work best if the yield curve is flat. Where the yield curve is upward or downward sloping, problems can arise. Macaulay duration is calculated on the basis that there is a parallel change in the yield curve, but this is rarely the case in reality. Short-term interest rates tend to move faster than long-term interest rates, and so there is not always a high degree of correlation between them. Duration in these circumstances cannot be guaranteed.

The duration gives an indication of how interest rate changes may affect an individual portfolio. This calculation is not always precise, making life a bit more difficult for the portfolio risk manager. Where the convexity is high the duration calculation will not be very accurate, and in extreme cases it may need to be recalculated on a daily basis.

Cash flow matching and dedication

One solution to the problems associated with immunization of a portfolio is to purchase zero-coupon bonds that provide payments in amounts exactly sufficient to match the projected cash outflow. Cash flow matching automatically immunizes the portfolio from interest rate movements. Portfolios using this strategy are referred to as dedicated portfolios. The advantage of a dedication is that it eliminates interest rate risk and thus eliminates re-balancing and possibly lowers transaction costs. Cash flow matching does pose some constraints, however. There may be more limitations on the bond selection process so that it can be impossible to pursue a dedication strategy using only 'underpriced' bonds. Also, if the portfolio to be cash flow matched is obligated to pay out a perpetual flow of income (as a pension fund is), that fund would have to purchase securities with maturities ranging for hundreds of years. Such securities do not exist.

Horizon analysis and riding the yield curve

Horizon analysis considers bond returns over a fixed time horizon as key influences on the price of the bonds are assumed to change. With this strategy, analysts or portfolio managers assess whether they think the current market price is too high or too low. Then they break down the return of a bond into the part due to the passage of time assuming no change in yields, and the part due to changes in yields assuming no passage of time. Once alternative bond returns have been considered over various time horizons given expected yields, the portfolio may be adjusted by swapping overpriced for underpriced bonds (bond swapping).

A particular version of horizon analysis is called **riding the yield curve**. This strategy involves buying higher-yielding longer-term securities than would be required to meet the cash outflow obligations, and selling them to obtain a capital gain when the outflow is due, assuming that the yield curve remains unchanged. For example, a fund manager with a liability due in three months could (i) buy a three-month bill which would mature on the date of the liability or (ii) buy a six-month bill and sell it after three months to meet the liability, which would yield an annualized return for the investor higher than that of the first option. This strategy only works if the yield curve is upward sloping and does not change in the meantime. Also, the strategy involves higher transaction costs since the portfolio manager has to buy and sell a security rather than just buying a security and holding that security to maturity.

Bond portfolio performance measurement

The performance of a bond portfolio can be measured by calculating the excess return to relative duration where the measure of risk is the duration, as follows:

$$\text{Excess return to relative duration} = \frac{r_p - r_f}{d_p/d_m}$$

where:

r_p = portfolio return
r_f = the risk-free return over the same period
d_p/d_m = the duration of the portfolio (d_p) relative to that of the market (d_m).

For example:

Portfolio	Portfolio return (%)	Portfolio duration (years)	Market duration (years)
A	10	16	8
B	8	8	8

Assuming the risk-free rate is 5%:

$$\text{Portfolio A} = \frac{10 - 5}{16/8} = 2.5$$

$$\text{Portfolio B} = \frac{8 - 5}{8/8} = 3.0$$

Thus, on a duration-adjusted basis, Portfolio B outperformed Portfolio A. Note that if the portfolio has the same duration as the market, then no adjustment is made to excess returns.

Quiz: Chapter 5

1   What is the current yield of a bond with a price of £85 and a coupon of £10?

  (A)   8.50%
  (B)   11.77%
  (C)   10.00%
  (D)   8.24%
  (E)   11.25%

2   What is the annuity factor for a bond with a semi-annual interest rate of 8% and a maturity of eight years? (Assume the bond is priced at par or 100.)

  (F)   10.63
  (G)   9.21
  (H)   21.82
  (I)   34.58
  (J)   30.32

3   _____ represents the rate of change of the slope of the price–yield curve.

  (A)   Duration
  (B)   Convexity
  (C)   Present value
  (D)   The discount rate
  (E)   Modified duration

4 Given the following table, what are the Macaulay duration and the modified duration?

	Coupon amount	Discount using 10%	Present value	PV × No. of years
1	15	0.9091		
2	15	0.8264		
3	15	0.7513		
4	15	0.6830		
5	15	0.6209		
6	15	0.5645		
7	15	0.5132		
8	15	0.4665		
9	15	0.4241		
10	115	0.3855		

(A) 5.71, 6.28
(B) 4.56, 7.98
(C) 7.98, 4.56
(D) 6.28, 5.71
(E) 5.01, 4.56

5 If the yield were to increase by 0.1% from 10% to 10.1% in the above example, given the modified duration formula, what would be the approximate change in bond price?

(A) 0.75
(B) 1.035
(C) 0.82
(D) 7.46
(E) 8.20

6 _____ is achieved by investing in a portfolio of bonds with similar duration as the duration of the existing stream of cash outflows.

   (A)   Macaulay duration
   (B)   Immunization
   (C)   Convexity
   (D)   Modified duration
   (E)   Discounting

7 Assuming the following, what are the excess returns relative to duration for A and B?

Portfolio	Portfolio return (%)	Portfolio duration (years)	Market duration (years)
A	20	10	6
B	10	5	6

rf = 4.5%

   (A)   10.1, 7.9
   (B)   7.9, 10.1
   (C)   9.3, 6.6
   (D)   8.9, 5.8
   (E)   5.8, 8.9

Chapter 6

Portfolio construction

This chapter focuses on the various facets of investment portfolio construction.

Building a portfolio

Rational investors wish to maximize the returns on their funds for a given level of risk. All investments possess varying degrees of risk. Returns come in the form of income, such as interest or dividends, or through growth in capital values (i.e. capital gains).

The portfolio construction process can be broadly characterized as comprising the following steps:

1 **Setting objectives**. The first step in building a portfolio is to determine the main objectives of the fund given the constraints (i.e. tax and liquidity requirements) that may apply. Each investor has different objectives, time horizons and attitude towards risk. Pension funds have long-term obligations and, as a result, invest for the long term. Their objective may be to maximize total returns in excess of the inflation rate. A charity might wish to generate the highest level of income whilst maintaining the value of its capital received from bequests. An individual may have certain liabilities and wish to match them at a future date. Assessing a client's risk tolerance can be difficult. The concepts of efficient portfolios and diversification must also be considered when setting up the investment objectives.

2 **Defining policy**. Once the objectives have been set, a suitable investment policy must be established. The standard procedure is for the money manager to ask clients to select their preferred mix of assets, for example equities and bonds, to provide an idea of the normal mix desired. Clients are then asked to specify limits or maximum and minimum amounts they will allow to be invested in the different assets available. The main asset classes are cash, equities, gilts/bonds and other debt instruments, derivatives, property and overseas assets. Alternative investments, such as private equity, are also growing in popularity, and will be discussed in a later chapter. Attaining the optimal asset mix over time is one of the key factors of successful investing.

3 **Applying portfolio strategy**. At either end of the portfolio management spectrum of strategies are active and passive strategies. An active strategy involves predicting trends and changing expectations about the likely future performance of the various asset classes and actively dealing in and out of investments to seek a better performance. For example, if the manager expects interest rates to rise, bond prices are likely to fall and so bonds should be sold, unless this expectation is already factored into bond prices. At this stage, the active fund manager should also determine the style of the portfolio. For example, will the fund invest primarily in companies with large market capitalizations, in shares of companies expected to generate high growth rates, or in companies whose valuations are low?

A passive strategy usually involves buying securities to match a pre-selected market index. Alternatively, a portfolio can be set up to match the investor's choice of tailor-made index. Passive strategies rely on diversification to reduce risk. Outperformance versus the chosen index is not expected. This strategy requires minimum input from the portfolio manager.

In practice, many active funds are managed somewhere between the active and passive extremes, the core holdings of the fund being passively managed and the balance being actively managed.

4 **Asset selection**. Once the strategy is decided, the fund manager must select individual assets in which to invest. Usually a systematic procedure known as an investment process is established, which sets guidelines or

criteria for asset selection. Active strategies require that the fund managers apply analytical skills and judgment for asset selection in order to identify undervalued assets and to try to generate superior performance.

5 **Performance assessment**. In order to assess the success of the fund manager, the performance of the fund is periodically measured against a pre-agreed benchmark – perhaps a suitable stock exchange index or against a group of similar portfolios (peer group comparison).

The portfolio construction process is continuously iterative, reflecting changes internally and externally. For example, expected movements in exchange rates may make overseas investment more attractive, leading to changes in asset allocation. Or, if many large-scale investors simultaneously decide to switch from passive to more active strategies, pressure will be put on the fund managers to offer more active funds. Poor performance of a fund may lead to modifications in individual asset holdings or, as an extreme measure, the manager of the fund may be changed altogether.

Types of assets

The structure of a portfolio will depend ultimately on the investor's objectives and on the asset selection decision reached. The portfolio structure takes into account a range of factors, including the investor's time horizon, attitude to risk, liquidity requirements, tax position and availability of investments.

The main asset classes are cash, bonds and other fixed income securities, equities, derivatives, property and overseas assets.

Cash and cash instruments

Cash can be invested over any desired period, to generate interest income, in a range of highly liquid or easily redeemable instruments, from simple bank deposits, negotiable certificates of deposits, commercial paper (short term corporate debt) and Treasury bills (short term government debt) to money market funds, which actively manage cash resources across a range of domestic and foreign markets. Cash is normally held over the short term pending use elsewhere (perhaps for paying claims by a non-life insurance company or for paying pensions), but may be held over the longer term as well. Returns on cash are driven by the general demand for funds in an economy, interest rates, and the expected rate of inflation. A portfolio will normally maintain at least a small proportion of its funds in cash in order to take advantage of buying opportunities.

Bonds

Bonds are debt instruments on which the issuer (the borrower) agrees to make interest payments at periodic intervals over the life of the bond – this can be for two to thirty years or, sometimes, in perpetuity. Interest payments can be fixed or variable, the latter being linked to prevailing levels of interest rates.

Bond markets are international and have grown rapidly over recent years. The bond markets are highly liquid, with many issuers of similar standing, including governments (sovereigns) and state-guaranteed organizations. Corporate bonds are bonds that are issued by companies.

To assist investors and to help in the efficient pricing of bond issues, many bond issues are given ratings by specialist agencies such as Standard & Poor's and Moody's. The highest investment grade is AAA, going all the way down to D, which is graded as in default.

Depending on expected movements in future interest rates, the capital values of bonds fluctuate daily, providing investors with the potential for capital gains or losses. Future interest rates are driven by the likely demand/ supply of money in an economy, future inflation rates, political events and interest rates elsewhere in world markets. As an example, UK gilt prices are influenced by price movements in US and German bonds.

Investors with short-term horizons and liquidity requirements may choose to invest in bonds because of their relatively higher return than cash and their prospects for possible capital appreciation. Long-term investors, such as pension funds, may acquire bonds for the higher income and may hold them until redemption – for perhaps seven or fifteen years. Because of the greater risk, long bonds (over ten years to maturity) tend to be more volatile in price than medium- and short-term bonds, and have a higher yield.

Equities

Equity consists of shares in a company representing the capital originally provided by shareholders. An ordinary shareholder owns a proportional share of the company and an ordinary share carries the residual risk and rewards after all liabilities and costs have been paid.

Ordinary shares carry the right to receive income in the form of dividends (once declared out of distributable profits) and any residual claim on the company's assets once its liabilities have been paid in full. Preference shares are another type of share capital. They differ from ordinary shares in that the dividend on a preference share is usually fixed at some amount and does not change. Also, preference shares usually do not carry voting rights and, in the event of firm failure, preference shareholders are paid before ordinary shareholders.

Returns from investing in equities are generated in the form of dividend income and capital gain arising from the ultimate sale of the shares. The level of dividends may vary from year to year, reflecting the changing profitability of a company. Similarly, the market price of a share will change from day to day to reflect all relevant available information. Although not guaranteed, equity prices generally rise over time, reflecting general economic growth, and have been found over the long term to generate growing levels of income in excess of the rate of inflation. Granted, there may be periods of time, even years, when equity prices trend downwards – usually during recessionary times. The overall long-term prospect, however, for capital appreciation makes equities an attractive investment proposition for major institutional investors.

Derivatives

Derivative instruments are financial assets that are derived from existing primary assets as opposed to being issued by a company or government entity. The two most popular derivatives are futures and options. *The extent to which a fund may incorporate derivatives products in the fund will be specified in the fund rules and, depending on the type of fund established for the client and depending on the client, may not be allowable at all.*

A **futures contract** is an agreement in the form of a standardized contract between two counterparties to exchange an asset at a fixed price and date in the future. The underlying asset of the futures contract can be a commodity or a financial security. Each contract specifies the type and amount of the asset to be exchanged, and where it is to be delivered (usually one of a few approved locations for that particular asset). Futures contracts can be set up for the delivery of cocoa, steel, oil or coffee. Likewise, financial futures contracts can specify the delivery of foreign currency or a range of government bonds.

The buyer of a futures contract takes a 'long position', and will make a profit if the value of the contract rises after the purchase. The seller of the futures contract takes a 'short position' and will, in turn, make a profit if the price of the futures contract falls. When the futures contract expires, the seller of the contract is required to deliver the underlying asset to the buyer of the contract. Regarding financial futures contracts, however, in the vast majority of cases no physical delivery of the underlying asset takes place as many contracts are cash settled or closed out with the offsetting position before the expiry date.

In actuality, futures are used by portfolio managers to better manage the returns of the underlying assets within the portfolio, such as equities and bonds. The advantages of financial futures include: (i) lower transaction costs compared to the underlying asset; (ii) greater liquidity than some of the underlying securities; (iii) the ability to take short positions and to leverage. For example, stock index futures can be used to hedge equity market risk. A UK fund manager can sell stock index futures on the FTSE in order to mitigate potential adverse movement in the UK equity market.

An **option contract** is an agreement that gives the owner the right, but not obligation, to buy or sell (depending on the type of option) a certain asset for a specified period of time. A call option gives the holder the right to buy the asset. A put option gives the holder the right to sell the asset. European options can be exercised only on the option's expiry date. US options can be exercised at any time before the contract's maturity date. Option contracts on stocks or stock indices are particularly popular. Buying an option involves paying a premium; selling an option involves receiving the premium. Options have the potential for large gains or losses, and are considered to be high-risk instruments. Sometimes, however, option contracts are used to reduce risk. For example, fund managers can use a call option to reduce risk when they own an asset. Only very specific funds are allowed to hold options.

Property

Property investment can be made either directly by buying properties, or indirectly by buying shares in listed property companies. Only major institutional investors with long-term time horizons and no liquidity pressures tend to make direct property investments. These institutions purchase freehold and leasehold properties as part of a property portfolio held for the long term, perhaps twenty or more years. Property sectors of interest would include prime, quality, well-located commercial office and shop properties, modern industrial warehouses and estates, hotels, farmland and woodland. Returns are generated from annual rents and any capital gains on realization. These investments are often highly illiquid.

The level of rents is driven by the general level of economic activity (specifically that in the local area of the property), plus the availability of similar property nearby. In the UK, institutional rental agreements often have terms of twenty-five years, with the tenant's rent often being subject to regular five-year, upward-only reviews.

Because of the prospects for rental growth, properties have historically been viewed as a reasonable long-term hedge against inflation.

The capital value of properties has been subject historically to changes in the level of interest rates and the economic cycle often going through cyclical peaks and troughs exacerbated by excessive bank lending to the sector.

Overseas assets

Markets, economies and companies across the world have different structures, prospects and strengths, and thus their price movements are not always correlated with one another. This creates overseas opportunities for active fund managers to maximize their returns whilst attempting to reduce portfolio risk.

UK fund managers usually have a highly international outlook and invest widely in foreign bonds, equities and properties. Besides providing diversification of risk, their investment decisions are driven by the relative prospects in share prices, inflation, interest rates and exchange rates in the particular overseas markets, when compared to those in the UK.

Passive versus active management

The two main portfolio management strategies utilized are passive management and active management. Sometimes portfolio managers will combine elements of both passive and active fund management. This technique is known as **portfolio tilting**. Here a fund manager might hold all the constituents of a particular index primarily in proportion to their market values within the index. However, a few constituents in, for example, the technology sector of the fund may be held in a proportion slightly higher than that in the index, and thus the portfolio is considered to be 'tilted' in the direction of technology stocks. One of the main difficulties in combining an active strategy with a passive strategy is in determining the degree to which the fund should be actively versus passively managed.

Passive fund management

A passive strategy usually involves holding a portfolio of assets for a long period of time (several years) with few changes over time, and entails little input from the fund manager. This strategy does not require the fund manager to outperform an index or to try to select undervalued assets. The theory behind passive fund management implies that two conditions are being satisfied in the securities market; efficiency and homogeneity of expectations. The assumption is that if securities markets are efficient, securities will always be priced fairly and there will be no incentive to trade actively. Also, if securities markets are characterized by investors who have homogeneous expectations of risks and returns, then again there is no incentive to trade actively. If too few securities are held in the portfolio, however, diversifiable risk may remain. Thus, a larger number of securities must be held for proper diversification.

One version of passive fund management that eliminates diversifiable risk is **index matching**, or **indexing**. Here, the fund manager attempts to match the selected index as closely as possible and to keep the fund positioned as such when money flows in and out of the fund. (Such funds are also known as tracker funds.) The passive fund management strategy has become increasingly popular as investors attempt to gain the return of the market index which is being tracked – no more and no less.

For bond portfolios that require liability matching (such as pension funds), two types of passive strategies are suitable:

- Immunization
- Cash flow matching.

Immunization is the name given to the technique used by fund managers that allows them to meet a promised stream of cash outflows with a high degree of certainty. Immunization is achieved by calculating the duration (the weighted average life of the bond) of the promised outflows, and investing in a portfolio of bonds with an identical duration. Provided the duration calculations are correct and there is no risk of major convexity (rate of change of the slope of the price–yield curve) adjustment, the danger of not having sufficient cash to meet a future commitment is limited. The duration of a bond portfolio is simply the weighted average of the durations of the individual bonds in the portfolio. Immunization may entail some re-balancing of the portfolio due to the erosion of duration over time.

Cash flow matching involves purchasing zero coupon bonds or other bonds that provide payments in amounts exactly sufficient to match the projected cash outflows. Portfolios using this strategy are referred to as dedicated portfolios. The advantage of dedication is that it eliminates interest rate risk and thus eliminates re-balancing and possibly lowers transaction costs. However, in practice it may be difficult to find bonds that exist with the appropriate maturity dates.

Active fund management

With an active fund management strategy, the portfolio manager constantly makes decisions and appraises the value of investments within the portfolio by collecting information, using forecasting techniques, and predicting the future performance of the various asset classes, market sectors, individual equities or assets. The goal is to obtain better performance for the portfolio. The fund manager uses personal ability and judgment to select under-valued assets to attempt to outperform the market.

Active fund managers do not believe that securities markets are always efficient. They believe that securities can be valued incorrectly by the market, thus giving rise to trading opportunities that can lead to excess returns. However, in practice, the amount of trading a fund manager will do in a fund may be limited by transaction costs. Timing the market in terms of buying and selling securities is also a part of active portfolio management.

Active managers running equity funds can adopt a number of strategies, all involving detailed analysis. Two common approaches are the 'top-down' and 'bottom-up' methods, which may be used singly or in combination to differing degrees.

The **top-down approach** involves assessing the prospects for particular market sectors or countries (depending on the index), following a detailed review of general economic, financial and political factors. To avoid underperforming the market, fund managers will often try to replicate the market sector and/or weightings. However, different sectors/countries move in and out of favour and so managers may go overweight in a sector/country if they like the prospects or underweight if they disagree with the market consensus. Sector weightings may be changed by fund managers depending on their view of the prevailing economic cycle (known as sector rotation). If a recession is likely, shares in consumer sectors such as retailing, homebuilders and motor distributors will be sold and the proceeds reinvested in, say, the food manufacturing sector. A portfolio is then selected of individual shares in the favoured sectors.

The **bottom-up approach** involves the careful selection of individual shares that are assessed to be relatively undervalued and are subsequently sold once they have been re-rated. This involves detailed analysis of available information including: reports on the markets in which the company operates, its competitive position; quality of management; products and technology; customer base and sales potential, prospects for exports; capital expenditure requirements; cost structure and supplier base; and an assessment of the strength of the balance sheet, income and cash flow statements. This analysis will then be combined with judgment on its relative share price, price earnings ratio, dividend prospects and market sentiment. The process may necessitate company visits and meetings with industry analysts. Using all this information, suitable forecasts can be drawn up and the decision made whether or not to buy.

With regard to active bond portfolio management, a bond portfolio can be constructed that will have less of a weighting in overpriced bonds and more of a weighting in underpriced bonds compared with the market portfolio. Also if, for example, a bond fund manager is expecting the market to rise because of a fall in interest rates, the manager will increase the duration of the portfolio by replacing low duration bonds with high duration bonds. Likewise, if expecting the market to fall because of a rise in interest rates, the fund manager will reduce the duration of the portfolio.

Two active bond portfolio management strategies that can be utilized are:

- Riding the yield curve
- Bond switching

Riding the yield curve involves buying higher-yielding longer-term securities than would be required to meet the cash outflow obligations and selling them to obtain a capital gains when the outflow is due, assuming that the yield curve remains unchanged. For example, a fund manager with a liability due in three months could (i) buy a three month bill that would mature on the date of the liability or (ii) buy a six-month bill and sell it after three months to meet the liability, which would yield an annualized return for the investor higher than that of the first option. This strategy will only work if the yield curve is upward sloping and does not change in the meantime.

Bond portfolio adjustments involve the purchase and sale of bonds or **bond switching**. The two main types of bond switches are anomaly switches and policy switches. In an anomaly switch, one bond is exchanged for another with very similar characteristics – i.e. maturity, coupon, and quality rating – but whose prices or yields are out of line with each other. In a policy switch, a switch is made between two dissimilar bonds. This is designed to take advantage of an expected change in interest rates, the yield curve, or bond quality ratings.

Asset allocation

To arrive at an asset allocation decision, the investor or fund manager must decide what mix of assets will give the required balance of risk and return. In theory, high risk asset allocation should give the greatest long-term returns; low risk allocation should give lower returns.

The main asset classes are cash, equities, bonds, property and overseas assets. To decide the right mix, the fund manager must consider: (i) the investor's objectives; (ii) the projected returns and risks attached to each asset class; and (iii) the correlation of returns between the asset classes (if interest rates go up, the value of bonds, equities and property usually fall and thus are positively correlated).

Asset allocation decisions will also invariably depend on the type of index against which a particular fund is measured. For a balanced fund, the primary allocation decision will be how much of the fund's weighting to put in bonds and how much in equities. For an international fund, the decision will involve how much of the fund's assets to invest in each of the countries specified by the benchmark index for that fund (i.e. where to go overweight and where to go underweight). If a fund manager is dealing with a single country fund, then the asset allocation decision will most likely be at the sector level. The portfolio manager can utilize various types of analysis, including fundamental and technical analysis to make asset allocation decisions in funds that are measured against benchmark indices.

Asset allocation – techniques

Over time a fund manager's expectations of risk and return may change, and by actively changing the asset mix the portfolio performance may be improved. **Tactical asset allocation** involves measuring the likely return on each asset class using suitable measures (e.g. yield on long bonds or economic indicators for equity markets) and shifting more funds into the asset class that is expected to outperform. Often, tactical deviation or bands for tactical asset allocation will be established. These are the range of weights around a benchmark or strategic weight in which a fund manager is allowed to invest. The bands will be narrower if the transaction costs are high, if the markets are excessively risky, or if the fund manager's skills are limited. An example of asset allocation tactical range is given in Table 6.1:

A fund manager can change the asset allocation of a fund by selling one asset class and buying another. A cheaper and faster way to achieve this goal, though, is to use the futures markets by buying or selling stock index or interest rate futures (if available). This avoids high transaction costs, and involves little time or disruption to the fund.

Table 6.1. Tactical asset allocation range (example)

Asset	Strategic weight	Tactical range (Weights)
Equities – domestic	70%	60%–80%
Equities – non-domestic	30%	25%–35%
Bonds – domestic	0	0–10%
Bonds – non-domestic	0	0–10%
Cash	0	0–10%

Another technique, **dynamic asset allocation**, is used to automatically adjust the asset mix in response to market movements. This technique involves buying stock index put options (options which give the buyer the right to sell the underlying index back to the writer at the agreed price) when the market is rising and selling them if the market falls in order to maintain the value of a portfolio at a certain level while maintaining the potential for higher returns. This strategy is sometimes referred to as portfolio insurance, or hedging – i.e. limiting risk by anticipating losses and gains that offset each other.

By using derivatives such as futures or options (whose value is *derived* from more conventional financial assets), a portfolio's performance can be enhanced, its risk level reduced, or its value protected. For example, buying call options (options that give the buyer the right to buy the relevant shares from the writer at the agreed price) in advance of cash flow receipts enables the fund to benefit in a rising market. The extent to which a fund can utilize derivatives will be defined in the fund's rules.

Asset allocation in practice

Fund management companies each decide on asset allocation differently. Some have small or large investment policy committees that meet monthly or weekly to consider the relative prospects for each asset class and the relevant economic and currency trends, and to determine the actual asset allocation decisions. Other companies allow individual investment teams to decide without much interference. The manner in which asset allocation is undertaken at a fund management company will depend largely on the culture of that company.

There is some debate as to how important asset allocation is in explaining portfolio returns. Some empirical evidence has shown that all securities within a single market tend to move in the same direction, but international markets and currencies do not. The conclusion from these studies is that the most important factor contributing to portfolio performance is choice of markets and currencies, not the individual securities.

Other studies point to costs as being a critical factor in fund performance. For example, assuming that the equity risk premium is 2.5% (market return equals 8.5% and risk-free rate equals 6%), if an equity fund carried a total cost of 2.5%, the investor would be indifferent in making the choice. There would be no premium for assuming the extra equity risk, as costs would have consumed 100% of the equity risk premium. That is, all of the costs of investing (such as advisory fees, other fund expenses, and transaction costs) take a bite out of the risk premium. Over time, returns of the portfolio are eroded by costs.

Stock selection

Once the asset allocation of a portfolio has been determined, stock selection can take place for the equity portion of the portfolio. Some funds (pure top-down funds) will decide only to apply asset allocation decisions and to leave the equities neutral versus the index. Other funds (pure bottom-up funds) will only deal with stock selection, and avoid asset allocation decisions versus an index completely. Most funds are somewhere in between, and apply a mix of asset allocation and stock selection in order to attempt to enhance returns as much as possible.

Valuation techniques

Equity prices are driven by the supply of and demand for the shares. Supply and demand for shares in turn are influenced by a variety of factors, including:

1 Economic and political outlook
2 Prospects for inflation and interest rates
3 Exchange rates
4 Company-specific factors
5 Growth potential in earnings per share and dividend yield.

Portfolio managers utilize a variety of simple and sophisiticated equity valuation techniques. One popular technique involves assessing a company's price/earnings (or P/E) ratio. The relative rating of a share, (whether it is cheap or expensive), is measured by its P/E ratio. A fund manager will buy a particular share if its prospective P/E ratio is relatively low and if he or she believes its earnings per share are likely to be higher than the market consensus. The formulas are given below:

$$\text{Earnings per share} = \frac{\text{Post tax profits available to ordinary shareholders}}{\text{Number of shares issued}}$$

$$\text{Price/earnings ratio} = \frac{\text{Market price per share}}{\text{Earnings per share}}$$

For example, a company achieves pre-tax profits of $3 m for the year to December 31, pays tax at 22%, and has 12 million ordinary shares in issue. The current market price of each ordinary share is $2.00. To calculate the earnings per share and P/E ratio:

$$
\begin{aligned}
\text{Earnings per share} &= \frac{\text{Post-tax profits}}{\text{Number of shares issued}} \\[2mm]
&= \frac{\$3\,m\ (1 - 0.22)}{12\,m} \\[2mm]
&= \frac{\$2.34\,m}{12\,m} \\[2mm]
&= 19.5 \text{ cents per share}
\end{aligned}
$$

$$
\begin{aligned}
\text{P/E ratio} &= \frac{\text{Market price}}{\text{Earnings per share}} \\[2mm]
&= \frac{\$2.00}{0.195} = 10.26
\end{aligned}
$$

All the above ratios can be calculated using historic and forecast figures. A P/E ratio of 10.26 needs to be compared with P/E ratios of other similar listed companies to see whether or not the share is relatively undervalued.

Another valuation method portfolio managers look at is EV/EBITDA, where:

EV = *Enterprise value* = Market capitalization + Net debt minus estimated value of 'non-core' assets

$EBITDA$ = Earnings before interest tax, depreciation, and amortization.

This ratio is used in a similar fashion to P/E ratios when attempting to find undervalued companies, and is particularly useful in comparing companies in the same sector but in different countries, which may have differing tax and accounting policies.

Another equity valuation technique involves looking at the discounted cash-flow values for companies being assessed, and comparing whether the current share price is above or below the fair value determined by discounting the future net cash flows of the company using a weighted average cost of capital. The valuation technique using dividend discount models states that the stock price should equal the present value of all expected future dividends in perpetuity. There will be more on dividend discount models and company financial ratios later in this book.

Equity valuation methods are continually evolving as the investment community constantly seeks to assess whether securities are over- or under-valued.

Optimization

Often during portfolio construction an optimization routine is used, which takes the judgments made from the information process and electronically builds a portfolio that most closely matches the investment goals. Optimization software products are often based on quadratic programming. In some cases the process mathematically determines the expected returns derived from the valuation model, with the risk of the portfolio derived from a risk model. In addition, a number of constraints can be placed upon the portfolio, which are then directly incorporated within the program and factored into the results. An optimization program may be used, for example, when a portfolio manager wants to select a subset of shares from a larger universe based on specific criteria – such as P/E ratios below a certain level and EPS growth rates above a certain level. An optimizer can then quickly select the appropriate shares from an existing database and display the appropriate portfolio based on the input conditions. Another example of usage of an optimization programme might occur when a portfolio receives an inflow of cash and the portfolio manager wants to know which share(s) to buy that would have the least impact on the portfolio's risk or beta. An optimization program can easily calculate the result based on the risk levels of the existing portfolio. These optimizers can be used for both asset allocation and stock selection purposes.

Quiz: Chapter 6

1 _____ occurs when a fund manager shifts assets into an asset class he or she expects to outperform in the future.

   (A) Dynamic asset allocation
   (B) Hedging
   (C) Bottom-up allocation
   (D) Tactical asset allocation
   (E) Indexing

2 _____ can be exercised only on that contract's expiration date.

   (A) A US options contract
   (B) A financial futures contract
   (C) A European options contract
   (D) A property contract
   (E) A derivatives contract

3 When a fund tracks an index as closely as possible, this is known as _____ .

   (A) passive fund management
   (B) convexity
   (C) active fund management
   (D) riding the yield curve
   (E) duration

4 With _____ , a fund manager holds a generally indexed portfolio apart from certain deviations with particular sectors or stocks.

   (A) immunization
   (B) index matching
   (C) optimization
   (D) dynamic asset allocation
   (E) portfolio tilting

5 _____ involves assessing which asset class is likely to outperform and then shifting more funds into that asset class.

(A) Dynamic asset allocation
(B) Tactical asset allocation
(C) Hedging
(D) Optimization
(E) Cash flow matching

6 The market expects a company to make pre-tax profits of £2 million for its next financial year ending on 31 December. If the company has 10 million shares in issue, pays tax at 33%, and the current share price is 201 p, what are the forecast earnings per share and the forecast P/E ratio?

(A) 13.4 p per share, 15
(B) 20 p per share, 10
(C) 10 p per share, 20
(D) 15 p per share, 13.4
(E) 200 p per share, 12

7 If a portfolio manager runs a computer program that selects a subset of shares with EV/EBITDA ratios below 5 and betas above 1, this is known as _____ .

(A) tactical allocation
(B) hedging
(C) dynamic allocation
(D) cash flow matching
(E) optimization

Chapter 7

Types of analysis

Active portfolio managers undertake a variety of different types of analysis in order to attempt to select outperforming equities for the portfolios they manage. The two extremes are fundamental analysis and technical analysis. Fundamental analysis focuses on the economic strengths and weaknesses of the market being assessed, and on the individual features of the stocks within the market. Technical analysis looks at patterns in the trading history of a particular market or stock to predict future price direction and levels. Usually portfolio managers will adamantly stick to one method of analysis, with the majority sitting in the fundamental analysis camp. Occasionally fund managers will combine the two approaches – fundamental analysis to determine the stocks and markets they wish to buy or sell, and technical analysis to determine the timing of the purchases and sales.

Fundamental analysis

For asset allocation purposes, fund managers will study the macro-economic environment in order to assess the direction of potential price movements of the different assets and markets in which their funds may invest. With stock selection, in addition to assessing the economic environment, fund managers will take into account the individual company's credit and operational risk along with details of its share price valuation.

Macro-economic considerations

When portfolio managers must choose in which countries within a regional portfolio to go over- or under-weight (asset allocation), they will often start with an assessment of the macro-economic conditions of the countries in the index being followed. Likewise, prospects for individual companies are tied to the broader economies in which they operate. As a result, it is important for fund managers and analysts to determine the state of the aggregate economy. The following are some of the indicators that they will examine:

- GDP growth
- Inflation rates
- Interest rates
- Trade accounts
- Current account balances
- Fiscal account balances
- Currency rates
- Unemployment levels
- Industrial production and manufacturing output data
- Proposed economic reforms
- Sovereign debt ratings
- Political issues and cycles.

Both the historic trends and attempted projections will be looked at to determine where in an economic cycle each country finds itself. This type of analysis may assist fund managers in both the selection and the timing of the proper countries within a fund. The analysis will also assist in determining the asset allocation to sectors within the countries. For example, a fund manager who notices that the currency in one country appears to be particularly undervalued may want to increase the asset weighting in this country (having screened the other macro parameters) in order to take advantage of a potential currency appreciation and subsequently enhanced currency-based returns for the portfolio. Another example of how macro-economic analysis might influence portfolio decisions is where interest rates are expected to decrease in a country. Under this scenario, portfolio managers may want to buy interest-rate sensitive sectors (such as banks) or companies (such as highly indebted corporations) within the portfolio.

Below, some of the more influential economic data points are reviewed.

Gross domestic product

Gross domestic product (GDP) is the most widely-used statistic to determine the overall health of an economy. GDP figures are typically produced quarterly or annually by government organizations. Preliminary estimates are given throughout the year, and these are subsequently revised. GDP measures the total production of an economy's goods and services. A high GDP growth figure indicates that an economy is growing rapidly, which, in turn, may mean that firms operating in that economy may have increased prospects for higher sales growth. The components of GDP are:

$$GDP = C + I + G + (X - M)$$

where:

C	=	consumption
I	=	investment
G	=	government spending
X	=	exports
M	=	imports
(X − M)	=	net exports.

Analysts often watch the different components of GDP closely because some of the components tend to provide a good indication of the future direction of the economy. Generally, GDP figures are adjusted for inflation by dividing the nominal GDP figure by a deflator (inflation rate adjustment). The resulting figure is the real GDP figure, which can be compared to historical figures. Industrial production is another popular measure of the condition of an economy. This statistic is a narrower measure of economic activity, and focuses only on the manufacturing side of the economy.

Interest rates

Interest rates affect the present value of future cash flows – high interest rates reduce the attractiveness of investment opportunities, and low interest rates increase the appeal of investment opportunities. A low interest rate environment is aimed at promoting business investment expenditures and, subsequently, higher growth rates. Mortgage payments and high-priced consumer durable goods such as automobiles are also sensitive to interest-rate movements. When interest rates are high, consumers spend less.

Inflation

Inflation is the rate at which the general price of goods rises. High rates of inflation are sometimes associated with economies that are growing too fast – where the demand for goods and services is outpacing productive capacity. The implication is that there will be an upward pressure on prices. Inflation expectations also lead to interest rate increases. The opposite of inflation is deflation, where prices spiral downwards. Deflation can put recessionary pressures on an economy as lower prices translate into lower profits for companies.

Employment

The unemployment rate is the percentage of the labour force that is actively looking for work. The unemployment rate measures the level to which an economy is operating at full capacity. A rising unemployment figure can point to a slowdown in the economy.

Budget deficit

The budget deficit of a government is the difference between government spending and government revenues. Shortfalls in the budget must be offset by government borrowing. If government borrowing is excessive, interest rates may be forced to go up and total demand for credit in the economy will increase. Higher interest rates are negative for business investment and, consequently, company growth.

Current account deficit

The current account is the difference between imports and exports, including merchandise, services, and transfers such as foreign aid. If the current account shows a deficit, this means that the country imports more than it exports; a surplus indicates that the country exports more than it imports. Current account deficits have to be funded somehow. Sometimes, foreign direct investment into a country will offset a current account deficit, or high interest rates may attract capital flow into a country. The level of the current account is affected by changes in the exchange rate. If a currency depreciates exports may increase, as it becomes less costly for foreigners to purchase domestically produced goods.

Exchange rates

The exchange rate is the rate at which domestic currency can be converted into foreign currency. Movements in exchange rates can affect the international competitiveness of domestically produced products. A sharp currency devaluation can lead to a rise in exports. Exchange rates can also have an effect on inflation rates. Depreciation of a currency increases the cost of imported goods, which results in an increase in local prices and consequently, the inflation rate.

Government policy

The government uses the tools of fiscal policy and monetary policy to promote GDP growth, regulate employment levels, and stabilize prices. These policies are described below.

Fiscal policy

Fiscal policy refers to the taxation and spending policies of the government designed to calibrate the economy. Government can stimulate growth in real GDP by creating tax incentives for investment. Likewise, increases in general tax rates immediately divert income from consumers and result in decreases in consumption. Decreases in government spending reduce the demand for goods and services. Fiscal policy is a direct way to stimulate or slow down an economy. One way to examine the net impact of a fiscal policy is to look at the government's budget deficit. If a large deficit is present, this means the government is spending more than it is taking in by the way of taxes. The net effect will be an increase in the demand for goods (through spending) by more than it reduces the demand for goods (through taxes). As a result, the economy will experience a push towards growth. Budget deficits are, however, associated with increased interest rates.

Monetary policy

Monetary policy refers to actions taken by a central bank to control interest rates and the money supply (the supply of money in the economy). Increases in the money supply lower short-term interest rates, subsequently encouraging investment and consumption demand. Over a longer period of time, however, many economists believe that a higher money supply will lead only to higher prices and inflation, and will not have a permanent effect on economic growth levels. Tools that the central bank has at its disposal include: buying and selling bonds for its own account to increase or decrease the money supply in the system; the interest rate charged to banks on short-term loans; and reserve requirements dealing with the amount of deposits that banks must hold as cash on hand or as deposits with the central bank. The ability of a central bank to maintain stable prices and interest rates whilst stimulating growth and maintaining a high level of employment is essential for providing an environment conducive to running profitable businesses.

The business cycle

Even though governments can use fiscal and monetary policies to attempt to keep inflation at bay and unemployment low, economies still repeatedly seem to pass through good and bad times. Analysts and fund managers must determine whether the economies in which they will invest are improving or deteriorating. A forecast that is wrong may have a negative impact on the investment strategy.

A business cycle incorporates periods of expansion and contraction of aggregate economic activity measured by the real GDP. The length and depth of the cycles can be irregular. Generally speaking, business cycles tend to last between six and ten years; however, this can be very difficult to forecast. The transition points across cycles are called peaks and troughs, with the high point of economic activity being the peak and the low point the trough. An economy is in an expansion phase between a trough and a peak, and in a contraction phase just after a peak and before a trough. Historically, periods of contraction have tended to be shorter than periods of expansion. Various types of cyclical indicators have been developed to help forecast the business cycle. Leading economic indicators (such as new orders for manufacturers) are indicators that tend to rise and fall with antecedence to the rest of the economy. Coincident and lagging indicators, such as industrial production and changes in the consumer price index, tend to move in tandem with or somewhat after the economy.

A practical look at macro-economic data

Portfolio managers often rely on external sources of economic data and forecasts to make informed decisions. They will have to be aware of any biases in the data that these sources may incorporate in their information, such as timeliness of change of estimates given new macro information available.

For example, given the data in Table 7.1, the following conclusions can be drawn:

1 Comparing GDP growth amongst the countries, between last year and this year, all the countries are expected to experience increased growth. Country Q in particular is expected to come out of a recession from −11.1% to 4.3%. This is probably due, in part, to the effects of the depreciation of its currency leading the trade balance to increase in positive terms.
2 It can be seen that the sharp devaluations of the currencies in Countries Q and R have led to inflation rates (CPI) being forecast to increase (quite dramatically, in the case of Country Q).
3 The current accounts as a percentage of GDP show that most of the countries in the region hold current account deficits (apart from Country Q). It would be necessary to analyse how these account deficits are being financed within each country in order to gauge how accurate the forecasts really are. In some cases the devaluation of the currency is causing the trade balances to improve, with exports surpassing imports.
4 Regarding the exchange rate movements, it can be seen that Countries Q and R have experienced sharp currency depreciations in recent years. The currencies of Countries S and T have shown milder devaluations. Further research would have to be done to see whether currency stabilization would, in fact continue past next year.

Table 7.1 Sample economic data and forecasts

Country		Country Q	Country R	Country S	Country T
	Economic activity				
GDP growth (%)	Four years ago	−3.4	0.8	−1.0	3.7
	Three years ago	−0.8	4.4	4.4	6.6
	Two years ago	−4.4	1.4	2.8	−0.3
	Last year E*	−11.1	1.4	1.8	1.1
	This year F*	4.3	2.0	3.3	3.0
	Next year F	5.0	3.0	4.5	3.7
	Prices				
CPI (Dec/Dec)	Four years ago	−1.8	8.9	2.3	12.3
	Three years ago	−0.7	6.0	4.5	9.0
	Two years ago	−1.5	7.7	2.6	4.4
	Last year E	41.1	12.5	2.8	5.7
	This year F	25.1	15.0	2.9	4.3
	Next year F	15.5	10.0	3.1	3.8
	Balance of payments				
Current account (USD Bn)	Four years ago	−11.9	−25.3	−0.3	−14.0
	Three years ago	−8.8	−24.6	−1.1	−18.2
	Two years ago	−4.4	−23.2	−1.2	−18.0
	Last year E	9.0	−9.3	−0.6	−15.0
	This year F	8.2	−7.3	−1.0	−17.9
	Next year F	5.0	−4.2	−1.3	−18.8
Current account (% GDP)	Four years ago	−4.2	−4.8	−0.4	−2.9
	Three years ago	−3.1	−4.1	−1.4	−3.1
	Two years ago	−1.7	−4.6	−1.9	−2.9
	Last year E	8.5	−2.1	−1.0	−2.3
	This year F	6.0	−1.7	−1.5	−2.8
	Next year F	2.9	−0.9	−1.8	−2.8
Trade balance (USD Bn)	Five years ago	−4.9	−6.6	−2.0	−7.9
	Four years ago	−2.2	−1.3	3.2	−5.6
	Three years ago	1.2	−0.8	2.2	−8.0
	Two years ago	6.3	2.6	2.1	−10.0
	Last year E	16.5	12.5	2.5	−8.1
	This year F	16.6	15.0	2.3	−10.1
	Fiscal accounts				
Fiscal balance (% GDP)	Five years ago	−1.4	−7.9	0.4	−1.5
	Four years ago	−2.6	−5.9	−1.4	−1.2
	Three years ago	−2.4	−4.5	0.1	−1.1
	Two years ago	−3.3	−3.6	−0.3	−0.7
	Last year E	−1.5	−3.5	−1.3	−0.7
	This year F	−0.6	−3.2	−0.8	−0.5
	USD exchange rate (year end)				
USD exchange rate	Five years ago	1.0	1.2	473.0	9.9
	Four years ago	1.0	1.8	529.3	9.5
	Three years ago	1.0	1.9	573.6	9.6
	Two years ago	1.0	2.3	661.0	9.1
	Last year E	3.4	3.5	720.0	10.4
	This year F	3.3	3.7	699.2	11.0
	Next year F	3.2	4.0	702.8	11.3

*E, estimate (even though the figures are for last year, final government produced figures may not be available yet); F, forecast

Source: Adapted from UBS Warburg Earlybird Report, March 2003.

The above exercise is just the beginning of macro-economic analysis that would be performed on a region or on countries. The next step would be to determine in which regions/countries to go over or underweight. Some fund management companies have macro-economic screens and templates that they superimpose on macro data to determine their asset allocation. Nonetheless the process must be dynamic, as new macro-economic data are disclosed weekly, monthly, and annually.

Industry life cycle

Many analysts believe that industries go through life cycles with respect to unit sales. There are several stages to the life cycle of an industry. At the beginning of the life cycle is the stage of early development, which is characterized by modest sales growth and very small or even negative profit margins and profits. Major development costs are incurred during this phase, as the market for the industry's product or services is still fledgling. Next is the phase of rapid growth and expansion, where a market develops for the product or service and demand becomes substantial. Little competition exists at this stage, and profit margins can be large. The industry builds productive capacity as sales grow and the industry attempts to meet excess demand.

The next phase is the mature growth phase. Here, the rapid growth of sales and the high profit potential attract competitors to the industry, which in turn causes an increase in supply and lower profit margins. The future sales growth may still be above the general average for the economy, but it is no longer accelerating. Profit margins begin to reach more normalized levels. Following the mature growth phase is the stabilization phase, where the rapid growth of sales and high profit margins attract competition into the industry. This causes an increase in supply and lower prices, and as a result profit margins begin to decline to normalized levels. Typically, the industry growth rate declines to match the growth rate of the aggregate economy or of the segment of the economy of which the industry is a part. Profit growth will vary from company to company and industry to industry.

The final stage of maturation involves deceleration of growth and decline of the industry. This stage of industry maturity is characterized by the industry's sales growth declining because of shifts in demand or growth of substitutes. Profit margins will be squeezed and some companies may experience losses. Investors may start to question the use of capital employed by the industry.

Industries in the early phases of their life cycles offer high-risk/high-reward investments. Industries that have recently reached maturity offer a low-risk/low-return investment strategy. Also, each industry is quite unique in how long it takes to progress through each phase. Some industries, such as the biotechnology industry, develop rapidly, whilst other industries, such as the natural gas industry, develop more slowly. External forces, such as political and regulatory changes, can influence a particular industry's progression through its life cycle. Social and democratic factors also play an important role in the development of an industry.

Example of model for analysis

Fundamental analysis for individual shares implies assessing the fundamentals not only of the company being considered, but also of the industry and sector in which it is situated. An analyst/fund manager would look closely at the balance sheet, income statement, and cash flow statement of the company being analysed. In order to determine earnings and cost projections, the analyst must be aware of the factors influencing (and expected to influence) the company and the sector. One of the frameworks often utilized for industry analysis is the Porter's Five Forces analysis, whereby the analyst looks at several features that might push or pull an industry and companies within that industry in a certain direction.

Figure 7.1 provides a summary of the basic Porter's Five Forces model. The application of this framework to each company/industry being analysed provides a systematic method of looking at the factors that might influence a company/industry positively or negatively. This information would be taken into consideration when finalizing a stock purchase or sale decision.

Power of suppliers	Rivalry	Power of the customer

Threats of new entrants

- Government regulation
- Competitive supply
- Access to distribution
- Competitor retaliation

Power of suppliers	**Rivalry**	**Power of the customer**
• Number of available suppliers • Substitution possibilities and cost of switching • Ease of backward integration	• Demand situation/cyclicality • Industry supply economics • Competitor behaviour • Government regulation	• Buyer price-sensitivity • Competitive pressures facing buyers • Buyer negotiating strengths • Availability of substitutes

Threat of substitution

- Substitutes' price advantages
- Customers' cost of switching
- Technical or price retaliation

Figure 7.1 Porter's Five Forces model

Sources of risk for equity

The required rate of return and risk premiums for a stock are based on several risks. Some of the most influential of these are listed below:

Business risk

Business risk is summarized by the variability of a company's profit margins based on the predictability of consistency of its earnings and sales. The higher the volatility of the profit margins, the higher the risk. This risk is sometimes also referred to as operating leverage. Both internal and external factors can affect a company's profits. To assess the risk from internal factors, it is necessary to look at the overall operating efficiency of the firm. Questions asked might ask include: Does the firm utilize the most effective mix of labour and capital? Do any expansion projects make sense? Is too much being spent on research and development?

External factors such as the price of oil or interest rate levels will affect certain companies. When oil prices are high for a sustained period of time, both oil companies and auto companies may be affected – whereas oil companies may benefit from higher revenues for the higher oil prices, auto companies may be negatively affected as people drive less and purchase fewer cars.

Therefore, the more sensitive the company's profits are to changes in prices and macroeconomic factors, the larger the firm's business risk. The business risk of a utility firm that supplies electricity will be smaller than the business risk of a bank, which is dependent on the level of interest rates prevalent.

Financial risk

Financial risk is the risk of insolvency, where the firm's total liabilities exceed total assets. Here, the riskiness of the firm's capital structure is measured. The degree of risk can be determined by the company's financial leverage or by the level of fixed charges relative to net income. Firms with a large amount of debt are riskier than firms that are financed primarily with equity. Consequently, the larger the proportion of debt obligations, the greater the financial risk for the firm. The firm's ability to meet interest and principal payments is a critical factor in determining the firm's financial risk.

Liquidity risk

Liquidity risk relates to poor marketability of a company's common stock. If the market for a company's assets becomes too thin to enable fair and efficient trading to take place, the liquidity risk will be deemed to be high. If the owner of an asset has difficulty in selling it when needed (no natural buyers in the market), he or she may have to offer the security at a price dramatically higher than the value of the asset to obtain the sale. For a bank, liquidity risk refers to the risk that the bank has insufficient funding to meet commitments as they arise. For other companies, the risk arises when the entity cannot meet payments when they fall due.

Agency risk

Agency risk is the risk that managers – agents of the company owners – will not act in the best interest of the firm. Managers might take a decision that would benefit themselves rather than the shareholders. For example, a manager might decide to open a branch office in a location closer to his or her home, rather than closer to the suppliers and customers. To avoid agency risk, firms try to align the interests of management with those of the shareholders. This is sometimes done by forcing the managers to hold a large number of company shares and/or share options.

Regulatory risk

Regulatory risk involves the possibility that new regulations imposed by government agencies may affect the operations of a company. For instance, a manufacturer could locate a factory in a certain area, only to find that the zoning laws change, disallowing any manufacturing in that area.

Interest rate risk

Interest rate risk arises from the impact of fluctuating interest rates, and will directly affect the firm's borrowing and investing of funds. Additionally, some investments may be exposed not only to the level of interest rates, but also to the shape of the yield curve (the trajectory between long- and short-term interest rates). Some types of institutions, particularly banks and highly leveraged companies, will be very sensitive to interest rate changes. Additionally, the investor's required rate of return will change as interest rates change.

Inflation risk

Inflation can cause distortions in the accounting measurement of a company's depreciation costs, inventory, and interest expense. For example, during periods of high inflation, depreciation values are understated relative to replacement costs and real economic income or cash flow is overstated. The same occurs with First In First Out (FIFO) inventory accounting. With high inflation, FIFO results in an overstatement of real income. The effect of inflation on interest is to understate real income.

Operational risk

Operational risk is the risk linked to non-financial matters, such as fraud, system failure, accidents, and breaches in corporate governance.

Currency risk

Currency risk arises from exposure to movements in foreign currency (FX) rates. This risk can be sub-divided into transaction risk, where currency movements affect the proceeds from day-to-day transactions, and translation risk, which affects the value of assets and liabilities on the balance sheet. Holdings within a fund in different currencies that appreciate or depreciate against the base currency in which the fund is quoted may have a positive or negative impact on the overall value of the fund.

Systematic risk

Systematic risk is the movement in securities that results from economic changes affecting the entire market. Market beta is the measure of systematic risk.

Technical analysis

Rather than looking at the fundamentals of the economy or of a company, technical analysts look at the patterns of share prices and trading history to determine the appropriate strategy to adopt. A technical analyst, often known as a chartist, monitors share price behaviour – the patterns of share prices and relationships between prices and other market data – and then, using historic information of recurring patterns, endeavours to select money-making stocks. Through the use of charts, technical analysts develop patterns of market behaviour that they expect can be repeated over and over again. To some extent, these predictions may be self-fulfilling. If the charts predict that a share price will fall and investment managers sell this share, then supply and demand factors will force the price of that share down. The technique is based heavily on recognizing past patterns, the supply and demand for a stock, investor psychology (the behaviour of crowds), and the use of certain mechanical rules. These rules include:

- The use of moving averages of share prices over time (often 20, 40 days or 200 days), trying to spot when a share has been over-sold and is due for an upwards price correction (or *vice versa*)
- Studying the number of daily price rises and falls and the number of shares traded on that day – a rise in price and volume indicates increasing investor interest which should continue
- Spotting support areas (prices at which investors will buy more shares) and resistance zones (prices at which investors will sell). For example, if a company issued shares at 100p a year ago and the price today is 90p, it is likely that a number of investors will sell once the price reaches 100p.

Dow theory

Most approaches to technical analysis assume that financial prices follow a market cycle model, where overall prices tend to move through long trends of either rising or falling price levels. The founder of one of the original trend theories was Charles Dow (founder of the Dow Jones news service), whose method, designed in the early 1900s, of analysing and interpreting stock market movement bears his name – the Dow Theory. The essence of the Dow Theory is that there are always three forces working on the stock market:

1 A primary or major trend akin to the tides in the ocean
2 A secondary reaction or intermediate trend that resembles waves
3 Daily fluctuations or short-term movements that resemble ripples.

The Dow Theory asserts that a bull market is established when both the Dow Jones Industrial Average and the Dow Jones Transportation Average are moving upwards. A bear market occurs when the indices are moving down. If one of the indices departs from the trend and is followed by a departure of the other index from the trend, then this is viewed as confirmation that the primary trend has changed. The basic tenets of the theory also purport that no additional information is required about the stock market outside of data on stock indices and that, usually, a positive relationship exists between the trend and volume of shares traded. The Dow Theory has been extended and changed over the years. However, most technical analysis theories stem from the Dow Theory.

Moving averages

Technical analysts study moving average charts in order to identify short- and long-term trends (as suggested by the Dow Theory). To construct a 30-day moving average chart, the arithmetic average of the prices from the previous 30 trading days would be taken. This calculation would be done every day by dropping the oldest day and adding the most recent day, thus creating a rolling or moving average. A technical analyst might compare the 200-day moving average to the 30-day moving average to contrast a long-term trend with a short-term trend. If the 200-day moving average was rising while the 30-day average was falling, one interpretation could be that price declines are expected in the short term, but not in the long term.

Moving averages can be used for market indices and for individual stocks. Technical analysts will look for moving average charts to cross each other to indicate a change in direction of a trend. Likewise, if prices of a stock or index reverse and break through or cross a moving average line from below on heavy volume, then this points to a strongly positive change. The indication is then that this breakthrough signals a reversal of a declining trend. The opposite would be true if prices crossed the moving average line from above.

Relative strength

Relative strength charts assess the performance of one company, industry or market relative to another. Typically, the relationship between two historical series of data is expressed as a ratio of one security or index divided by another security or index. For example, a technical analyst may want to compare the performance of a particular share to overall market performance. The share price may have shown a trend of outperformance compared to the index over a given period of time.

The **relative strength indicator** (RSI) measures the relative internal strength of a price pattern and is a percentage ranging from 0% to 100%. Typically, a reading of 30 or less indicates an oversold condition, while a reading of 70 or above points to an overbought situation. The actual numerical calculation for RSI is rather complex, and most data services, such as Bloomberg provide the calculations. The best signals are noted when the

RSI enters overbought or oversold areas and begins to pull back. Here, it could be deduced that the price movement has reached an extreme and is likely to reverse soon. Alternatively, some technical analysts believe that high RSI figures signify an ongoing trend and consequently a buy signal (the trend is your friend). In this case, the analyst will only sell after the RSI has fallen significantly.

Market breadth indicators

Several technical indicators exist that are believed to be leading indicators of future direction in price movement of a security or index. These indicators can be classified into breadth or sentiment indicators.

Breadth indicators highlight overall market strength or weakness. The following are some examples of momentum indicators, or breadth indicators.

The advance–decline line

The advance–decline line is a cumulative measure of how many stocks are up for the day on an exchange relative to how many stocks are down for the day. For example, given the information for a particular week (see Table 7.2), the advance–decline line can be calculated.

In Table 7.2, the difference between the advancing and declining issues is taken and the cumulative sum is then calculated. On Wednesday, more issues declined than advanced, and the cumulative advance–decline for that day was: −550 + 200 = −350.

Table 7.2 Advance–decline line (example)

Day of the week	Advancing issues	Declining issues	Difference	Cumulative
Monday	1000	1150	−150	−150
Tuesday	900	1300	−400	−550
Wednesday	1200	1000	+200	−350
Thursday	1340	850	+490	+140
Friday	1100	1075	+50	+190

The cumulative advance–decline figures can then be plotted to create the advance–decline line. Most technical analysts view a falling advance–decline line in a rising market as a bearish warning signal, and a rising advance–decline line in a falling market as a bullish sign.

52-week new high/new low ratio

This category of breadth indicator compares 52-week new highs and 52-week new lows, where the new high is expressed as a percentage of (new highs + new lows). The raw ratio can sometimes be volatile, but if a 10-day and 25-day moving average is applied, the change in trend indicator becomes more useful. When the 10-day moving average crosses over the 25-day moving average in a counter-swing fashion, particularly after sharp moves when the 10-day moving average greatly exceeds the 25-day moving average, the result is a fairly strong buy or sell signal.

Sentiment indicators

Sentiment indicators attempt to gauge the overall mood and prevailing psychology of the general marketplace. Sentiment indicators can confirm general trends, but can also determine when a trend is likely to reverse soon. As a result they become most indicative when they reach extreme levels, where the assumption is made that the market is about to exhaust itself and that the prevailing trend is likely to change. When sentiment indicators are used in this way, they are known as contrary indicators. The idea is that the crowd is usually wrong at significant market turning points. There are many sentiment indicators, including:

- Put/call ratio
- Cash balances held by mutual funds or unit trusts
- Credit balances held by brokerage accounts
- Consensus estimates
- Short-selling data
- Odd-lot trading
- Directors' dealings.

Some of these are discussed below.

Put/call ratio

The put/call ratio is probably the most widely used sentiment indicator. The ratio is calculated by dividing the volume of put option trading by the volume of call option trading. Excessive put buying or a high ratio is viewed as a bearish signal, and excessive call buying or a low ratio is considered bullish. Investors buy put options (the right to sell stocks in the future) when they believe that the stock prices will fall, and call options (the right to buy stocks in the future) when they believe prices will rise. Typically, the volume for call options is greater than the volume for put options, and the indicator will usually be below 1.0 (or less than 100%). Put/call ratios may be calculated for most indices.

Consensus estimates

Various agencies conduct polls of the investment community asking for evaluations of various markets, including the stock market. These polls are usually conducted weekly and published the following week. The data obtained from these polls are used as contrary indicators. When the investment community becomes excessively bullish, technical analysts become more cautious. Conversely, when the investment community becomes more bearish, the technical analysts become more bullish. The same analysis could be performed by comparing the number of stock market newsletters that are positive to those newsletters that are negative.

Directors' dealings

Corporate officers or main shareholders of a company that hold more than 5% of the total voting stock of a company are known as 'insiders'. They are required to file with the Securities and Exchange Commission (SEC) or other local stock authorities, their sales and purchases. Generally, insiders are fairly accurate in their buying and selling decisions because of their intimate knowledge of the company. Also, they are in the best position to assess their company's relative value in the marketplace. Thus company directors tend to sell before their stock hits the top and buy before their stock completes a bottoming phase. One caveat, though: insider buying tends to be more accurate than insider selling. Sometimes a director may sell shares to raise cash for personal reasons, such as to fund a child's education or to buy a new home. A strong positive signal is set when a number of insiders are buying significant volumes of their company stock. When insiders are selling considerable volumes of their company stock, this should be a cause for concern.

Charts

Technical analysts plot market data in charts, such as bar charts, point-and-figure charts, and candlestick charts, to make inferences about future prices. Bar charts show each day's, week's or month's high, low and closing price movements for a designated time period. Point-and-figure charts distinguish reversals in the stock price direction. These charts comprise of a series of *x*'s and *o*'s positioned within a grid. The *x*'s represent price increases over a specified amount, and the *o*'s represent price decreases over a specified amount. Candlestick charts were originally developed in Japan and are similar to bar charts, but also include opening and closing prices.

Some examples of often-used technical analysis charts are given below.

Trends

A trend is the direction in which a share price is heading. Three choices of trend exist:

1 Positive or advancing trend
2 Negative or declining trend
3 Neutral or sideways trading range.

Assessing prevailing trends is important, because positioning trades with the trend tends to make most money – i.e. buying in up trends and selling in down trends.

A **positive trend** (see Figure 7.2) is characterized by higher highs and higher lows.

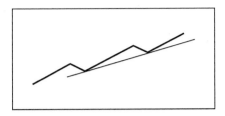

Figure 7.2 Positive trend

Consolidation patterns

Prices do not usually continue straight up or straight down for very long. Corrections within the major trend usually occur, which will then carry prices either sideways or slightly against the trend. These interruptions are known as consolidations, because share price patterns pause to consolidate the gains or losses. Consolidation patterns are generally known as continuation patterns because they usually indicate that prices will continue to move in the overall direction of the major trend, after a short pause. Often, there is a noticeable drop in volume during the pause.

Triangles (Figure 7.3) are drawn from very short-term trend lines connecting the relevant tops and bottoms of very short-term price swings

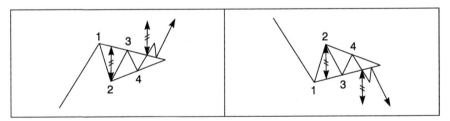

Figure 7.3 Triangles

Reversal patterns

Reversal patterns are transition areas in which market tendencies begin to shift from bullish to bearish or *vice versa*. The volume of shares being traded during this period usually helps to identify the phase of the reversal formation.

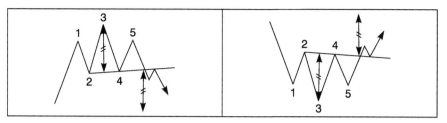

Figure 7.4 Head and shoulders

Head and shoulders (see Figure 7.4) – the most reliable reversal pattern – occurs as either a head and shoulders top or head and shoulders bottom.

Summary

The above are just some of the types of technical analysis performed by analysts and fund managers. Optimally, technical analysis involves a great deal of scientific concepts and discipline. In practice, not all analysts have access to the software needed to do the full optimization necessary. However, many current pricing systems, such as Bloomberg, do offer some of the basic technical analysis charts on most equities. It must be realized that technical analysis indicators are merely tools to help fund managers and analysts predict price movements, and that their reliability varies over time. They can be used as inputs in a wider context of stock analysis, including fundamental analysis, to assist in stock selection and timing.

Quiz: Chapter 7

1 High rates of _____ are sometimes associated with economies that are growing too fast – where the demand for goods and services is outpacing productive capacity.

   (A) interest
   (B) employment
   (C) foreign exchange
   (D) budget deficits
   (E) inflation

2 Increasing general tax rates is a tool used in _____ .

   (A) fiscal policy
   (B) exchange rate control
   (C) monetary policy
   (D) employment balancing
   (E) currency depreciation

3 During the _____ of the industry life cycle, competition is attracted into an industry, causing profit margins to normalize.

   (A) maturation phase
   (B) mature growth phase
   (C) rapid growth phase
   (D) expansion phase
   (E) stabilization phase

4 Analysis of an industry or sector shows that new technology about to be launched would make it cheaper for a customer to move into using this newer technology rather than the existing, more conventional method. Under Porter's Five Forces model, this would be called _____ .

   (A) threat of new entrants
   (B) power of the customer
   (C) rivalry
   (D) power of the suppliers
   (E) threat of substitution

5 Breaches in corporate governance would be an example of
_____ .

(A) systematic risk
(B) operational risk
(C) liquidity risk
(D) regulatory risk
(E) interest rate risk

6 The _____ is a percentage measuring the internal
strength of a price pattern.

(A) resistance level
(B) moving average
(C) RSI
(D) support level
(E) volume peak

7 The _____ occurs when a price reaches a certain point
from which, technically, it is expected to move downwards.

(A) resistance level
(B) consolidation pattern
(C) triangle
(D) volume peak
(E) support level

8 _____ are probably the most reliable reversal patterns
in technical analysis.

(A) triangles
(B) resistance levels
(C) head and shoulders
(D) support levels
(E) volume peaks

Chapter 8

Valuation methodologies – shares

How does an investor determine whether or not a share is fairly valued or represents a bargain investment? Many investors rely on values obtained from various valuation techniques to make investment decisions and to interpret financial information. Some theorists claim that stock prices cannot be predicted, particularly in the short term, and that no stock valuation model can accurately uncover under- or overpriced stocks. Nonetheless, it is important for fund managers and analysts to have some sort of consistent methodology with which to rank a universe of shares. Also, if the market is using a particular valuation technique, the 'herd mentality' could affect the prices of the underlying shares. Thus it is useful to be aware of some of the most popular valuation methods currently utilized.

Stock valuation methodologies can either be based on the discounted cash flow (DCF) principle, which states that the current value of an asset is the present value of all its future cash flows, or on financial ratio analysis. Using discounted cash flows involves forecasting future cash flows and estimating the appropriate discount rate to use for the calculation. With DCF, it is possible to establish whether a stock is undervalued, fairly or overvalued:

If the PV > P_0, investors would buy the stock
If the PV < P_0, investors would not buy the stock
If the PV = P_0, investors would be indifferent to buying or not

where PV is the present value of the expected cash flows and P_0 is the current share price.

Price ratio analysis, however, is more widely used by financial analysts than discounted cash flow models, and can be considered easier to calculate by the general public. Both methodologies are covered in this chapter.

Dividend discount model

One widely used method to value common stock is the dividend discount model (DDM), which values a share as the sum of all its expected future dividend payments, with the dividends adjusted for risk and the time value of money. The formula is as follows:

$$V_0 = \frac{D_1}{(1 + k)} + \frac{D_2}{(1 + k)^2} + \frac{D_3}{(1 + k)^3} + \ldots + \frac{D_t}{(1 + k)^t}$$

where:

D_t = the dividend to be paid t years from now
V_0 = the present value of the future dividend to be paid t years from now
k = the appropriate risk-adjusted discount rate.

This formula assumes that the last dividend is paid t years from now and the value of t depends on the specific situation being considered.

For example, suppose that a stock pays three annual dividends of 100p per year and that the discount rate is k = 7%. What is the present value of the stock?

$$V_0 = \frac{100p}{(1.07)} + \frac{100p}{(1.07)^2} + \frac{100p}{(1.07)^3} = 262.43p$$

Thus, the stock price should be valued at about 262p per share.

Constant dividend growth rate model

The constant dividend growth rate model is another common valuation model utilized to determine a stock's value as well as a firm's cost of equity. This model assumes that dividends will grow at a constant growth rate. By letting a constant growth rate be denoted by g, then successive annual dividends are stated as:

$$D_{tH} = D_t(1 + g)$$

For example, if the first dividend D_1 = 100p and the dividend growth rate g = 10%, then the second dividend payment would be D_2 = 100p × 1.10 = 110p. The third dividend payment would equal D(3) = 100p × 1.10 × 1.10 = 100p × (1.10)^2= 121p. Assuming the discount rate is k = 8%, the present value of the three dividend payments is the sum of their separate present values:

$$V_0 = \frac{100p}{(1.08)} + \frac{110p}{(1.08)^2} + \frac{121p}{(1.08)^3} = 283p$$

Usually the number of dividends to be paid is large and calculating the present value of each dividend separately is time consuming. However, if the growth rate is constant, some simplified formulas are available to handle certain special cases. If, for example, a stock pays annual dividends over the next t years and these dividends are expected to grow at the constant growth rate g and to be discounted at the rate k, then the calculation is as follows:

Current dividend $\quad$ = D_0
Dividend at time 1 $\quad$ = D_1 = D_0 (1 + g)
Dividend at time 2 $\quad$ = D_2 = D_1 (1 + g)
etc.

The present value of the next t dividends following D_0, can be calculated using the following formula:

$$V_0 = \frac{D_0 (1 + g)}{k - g} \left[1 - \left(\frac{1 + g}{1 + k} \right)^t \right]$$

where g does not equal k.

For example, assume that the growth rate is 6% and that the discount rate is 12%. If the number of annual dividends is 10 and the current dividend is 10p, what is the present value calculation?

$$V_0 = \frac{10p (1.06)}{0.12 - 0.06} \left[1 - \left(\frac{1.06}{1.12} \right)^{10} \right] = 74.8p$$

Constant perpetual growth model

A simplified version of the constant dividend growth rate model occurs when dividends are expected to grow at the constant rate g in perpetuity. The constant perpetual growth model is calculated using the following formula:

$$V_0 = \frac{D_0\,(1 + g)}{k - g}$$

where $g < k$.

Since $D_0\,(1 + g) = D_1$, the constant perpetual growth model can be written as:

$$V_0 = \frac{D_1}{k - g}$$

where $g < k$.

Thus the constant dividend growth model demonstrates that the value of a stock is the first year dividend per share, divided by the discount rate, minus the constant growth rate. The greater the growth rate, all other factors being equal, the larger the discounted future dividends will be, resulting in a higher share price. With this model, future dividends do not have to be estimated directly; only the growth rate has to be estimated.

Also, this formula only holds true when the growth rate is lower than the discount rate. If the growth rate were higher than the discount factor, the dividends would grow faster than the discount rate. The discounted cash flow of an infinite stream of dividends would yield an infinite price which would not be viable. Also, another limitation of the model is that it should only be applied to companies that have stable earnings and dividend growth.

For example, a certain company's dividends are projected to grow at 5% forever. If the discount rate is 12%, and the current dividend is $20, what is the value of the stock?

$$V_0 = \frac{\$20\,(1.05)}{0.12 - 0.05} = \$300$$

Thus, the stock should be priced at $300.

Estimating sustainable growth rates

When using the constant perpetual growth model, it is essential to establish an estimate of the growth rate (g) in dividends. There are a few ways of estimating the g – such as using the company's historical average growth rate, or using an industry median or average growth rate. In addition, a company's earnings growth rate can be used to estimate g. Usually the earnings per share (EPS) and the dividends per share (DPS) grow concurrently. However, the EPS may increase or decrease over time, making it difficult to estimate accurately. The focus is on the growth rate of the dividends for the model, because they represent the cash flows that the investors actually receive.

A company's earnings can be paid out as dividends to its shareholders or the earnings can be kept within the firm to finance future growth The portion of the earnings paid out as dividends is known as the payout ratio and the portion of the earnings retained within the firm is known as the retention ratio. Firms grow by reinvesting the retained earnings. If a company pays fewer dividends and increases the amount invested in profitable projects, higher future earnings should ensue. Such a company will achieve growth in earnings and dividends. The lower the proportion of earnings paid out as dividends, the greater the company's future growth rate.

The payout ratio is equal to $\dfrac{D}{EPS}$

where D = dividends
and EPS = earnings per share.

What is not paid out is retained, and the retention rate $= \dfrac{1 - D}{EPS}$.

For example, if a company's current dividend is 5p per share and its EPS is currently 12p, then the payout ratio is 5p/12p = 42%. The retention ratio is 1 – 0.40 = 0.58, or 58%.

A company's sustainable growth rate is equal to its return on equity (ROE) times its retention ratio:

Sustainable growth rate = ROE × Retention ratio

= ROE × (1 – Payout ratio)

The calculation for return on equity is as follows:

ROE = net income/Equity

Below are a couple of examples.

For example, Company A has a return on equity (ROE) = 6.8%, earnings per share (EPS) = $1.36 and a share dividend of D_0 = $1.05. Assuming a 7.5% discount rate, what is the value of Company A's stock?

$$\text{Payout ratio} = \frac{\$1.05}{\$1.32} = 0.80, \text{ or } 80\%.$$

Retention ratio = $1 - 0.80 = 0.20$, or 20%.

Company A's sustainable growth rate = $0.20 \times 6.8\% = 0.0136$, or 1.36%.

Using the constant growth model

$$V_0 = \frac{D_0 (1 + g)}{k - g}$$

the value of the stock is calculated as:

$$V_0 = \frac{\$1.05(1.0136)}{(0.075 - 0.0136)} = \$17.33.$$

This estimated value of the share can be compared to the actual price at which Company A's shares are trading in the market. If the value determined by the constant growth model is lower than the market price, then it can be assumed that Company A's stock may be overvalued, but it could also mean that a 1.36% growth rate underestimates the company's future dividend growth.

Again for example, Company B has an ROE of 10%, EPS of $2.15, and a dividend per share D_0 of $1.40. First calculate the retention ratio and the sustainable growth rate, then calculate the value of Company B's stock using a discount rate of 8.00%.

$$\text{The dividend payout} = \frac{\$1.40}{\$2.15} = 0.651, \text{ or } 65.1\%.$$

Retention ratio $= 1 - 0.651 = 0.349$, or 34.9%.

Company B's sustainable growth rate $= 0.349 \times 10\% = 3.49\%$.

Using this data in the perpetual growth model, the value for the share can be calculated.

$$V_0 = \frac{\$1.40(1.0349)}{(0.80 - 0.0349)} = \$32.13.$$

This value can be compared to the actual share price to determine whether the stock is over- or undervalued.

The limitation with sustainable growth rates is that they are sensitive to fluctuations in earnings. Fund managers and analysts will usually adjust sustainable growth rate estimates to smooth out the effects of earning oscillations. However, there is no standard method of adjusting growth rates, and analysts and fund managers depend on personal experience and their own judgment to fine tune the growth rates within their models.

The two-stage dividend growth model

In reality, companies do not experience just one growth rate throughout their life cycle, but may experience temporary periods of unusually high or low growth. Also the company's growth rate will probably eventually converge to an industry- or economy-wide average. For example, firms involved in the research and development of a new pharmaceutical product can achieve higher than average growth or supergrowth for a limited period of time. If the company's research is successful, the company can obtain a patent on the product for a limited number of years, during which the high growth prevails. For companies experiencing varied growth rates, the two-stage dividend growth model is utilized. To determine the proper value of the stock, dividends must be discounted by the applicable growth rate for the specified periods. The company will have one growth rate for one period and another growth rate after that.

The two-stage dividend growth model (also known as the multi-stage dividend discount model) can be written as follows:

$$V_0 = \frac{D_0 (1 + g_1)}{(1 + k)} + \frac{D_1 (1 + g_2)}{(1 + k)^2} + \frac{\left(\dfrac{D(2) (1 + g_2)}{(k - g_2)} \right)}{(1 + k)^2}$$

where:

V_0 = value of the stock
D_1 = next period's estimated dividend based on the company's growth rate in dividends
k = required rate of return or discount rate
g_1 = company's growth rate in stage 1
g_2 = company's growth rate in stage 2.

For example, Company C pays an annual divided of $1.00 and has a dividend growth rate of 10% per annum. Assuming the growth rate in dividends is expected to drop to 6% per starting in year 3 and the required rate of return on the stock is 7%, calculate the value of the stock using the two-stage dividend growth model.

At the end of year 2, the company's following year growth rate becomes 8% and

D_1 = ($1.00 × 1.10) = $1.10
D_2 = ($1.10 × 1.10) = $1.21
D_3 = ($1.21 × 1.06*) = $1.28

* At the end of year 2, next year's growth rate becomes 6% and
    $D_3 = D_2 × 1.06$.

Using the formula, the value of the company's stock is:

$$V_0 = \frac{\$1.10}{1.07} + \frac{\$1.21}{(1.07)^2} + \frac{\left(\dfrac{\$1.28}{(0.07 - 0.06)}\right)}{(1.07)^2}$$

$$= \$1.03 + \$1.06 + \frac{\$128}{(1.07)^2}$$

$$= \$1.03 + \$1.06 + \$111.80 = \$113.89$$

The longer the number of years that a firm can enjoy extraordinary profits, the bigger the expected jump in the stock price due to the availability of these profitable projects. The original dividend growth formula can be adjusted for a stock with a higher growth rate for t years and normal growth thereafter, as follows:

$$V_0 = \frac{D_0 (1 + g)}{k - g} \left[1 - \left(\frac{1 + g_1}{1 + k}\right)^t \right] + \left(\frac{1 + g}{1 + k}\right)^t \frac{D_0(1 + g_2)}{k - g_2}$$

In this formula, the first part of the equation measures the present value of the dividends through time t and the second part of the equation measures the present value of the subsequent dividends.

For example, suppose that a company has a current dividend of $2, and that dividends are expected to grow at the rate of $g_1 = 10\%$ for $t = 6$ years and thereafter at the rate of $g_2 = 5\%$. With a discount rate of $k = 7\%$, what is the present value?

$$V_0 = \frac{\$2(1.10)}{0.07 - 0.10} \left[1 - \left(\frac{1.10}{1.07}\right)^6 \right] + \left(\frac{1.10}{1.07}\right)^5 \frac{\$2(1.03)}{0.07 - 0.03}$$

$$= \$13.23 + \$60.79 = \$74.03$$

A requirement for the two-stage growth formula is that the second stage growth rate is strictly less than the discount rate and that $g_2 < k$. However, the first stage growth rate g_1 can be greater than, smaller than, or equal to the discount rate.

Estimating the discount rate or cost of equity capital

The discount rates used in the examples above come from the Capital Asset Pricing Model (CAPM). To review,

Discount rate $=$ Risk-free rate $+$ (stock beta $\times$ stock market risk premium)

In actuality, the discount rate is the cost of equity capital required by the stockholders given the firm's risk. The constant dividend growth model can be used to estimate the cost of equity. The assumption in this case is that the stock price is fairly valued and the formula solves for the discount rate k. The constant dividend growth model provides the following:

$$V_0 = \frac{D_1}{k - g}$$

which can be rewritten as

$$k = \frac{D_1}{V_0} + g$$

The values for D_0 and V_0 can be found in the market. If g can be estimated, $D_1 = D_0 (1 + g)$ can be calculated and it is possible to solve for the required cost of equity. This represents the expected rate of profit on the equity. Using an example that relates to the constant growth model (not two-stage growth model), where:

D_1 $\$5$
$V_0 = \$100$
$g = 5\%$

thus

$$k = \frac{\$5}{\$100} + 0.05 = 0.05 + 0.05 = 0.10$$

$$= 10\%$$

The investors who determine the stock price in the market are requiring a return of 10% on their investment. If a particular investor's required rate of return is more than 10%, then that investor should steer clear of buying or investing in that stock. If the investor's rate of return is lower than 10%, than this stock provides an attractive investment.

Free cash flow approach

One assumption made with the dividend discount approach to share valuation is that retained earnings are the only source of financing of new equity investment in the firm. The results may be affected if external equity financing plus debt financing of new investments were allowed. The principle behind the free cash flow approach to valuing stocks is that the intrinsic value of the equity in a firm is the present value of the net cash flows to shareholders that can be created by the company's existing asset base plus the net present value of investments that will be made in the future.

The free cash flow model estimates the value of the firm as a whole, and derives the value of the equity by subtracting the market value of the non-equity claims. The estimate of the value of the firm is found by calculated the present value of the cash flows, assuming the firm is financed only by equity, and then adding the present value of tax shields created by using debt if applicable.

In the model,

Free cash flow to equity (FCFE) = Net income

+ Depreciation expense

− Capital expenditure requirements (CAPEX)

− Change in working capital requirements

− Principal debt repayments

+ New debt issued

A reduced form of the dividend discount model can be used to determine the value of equity from the FCFE model:

$$V_e = \frac{\text{FCFE}\ (1 + g)}{k_e + g}$$

where:

V_e = value of equity
FCFE = expected free cash flow to flow to equity in year 1
g = expected growth rate
k_e = cost of equity capital

For example, assuming that Company D has 1 million common shares outstanding and no preferred shares, that cost of equity is 8% and the growth rate is 3%, calculate the value of equity from the FCFE given the information in Table 8.1.

Table 8.1 FCFE (example)

Net income	$10 000 000
Depreciation	1 000 000
CAPEX	2 000 000
Change in working capital	3 000 000
Repayment	1 000 000
New debt	4 000 000
Total FCFE	9 000 000
Total FCFE per share	$9.00

Using the formula described above:

$$V_e = \frac{9\,000\,000(1.03)}{0.10 - 0.03}$$

$$= 132\,428\,571, \text{ or } \$132.43 \text{ per share.}$$

This is a simple example using the discounted cash flow approach. In corporate finance, this approach is expanded upon to determine the values of companies for merger and acquisition purposes. The discount rate or weighted average cost of capital (WACC) will equal the weighted average cost of equity plus the weighted average cost of debt. Some analysts also use the expanded DCF model to ascertain share value.

Price ratio analysis

Although purists will recommend the discounted cash flow methods to evaluate share value, price ratios are also widely used by the investor community. Price ratios are simpler to calculate and more available to the amateur investor. Often fund managers and analysts will use price ratios in combination with discounted cash flow share analysis, as no single valuation method is necessarily appropriate or adequate for all occasions. A few of the popular price ratio methods are reviewed below.

Price to earnings ratio

Undoubtedly the most popular price ratio used to assess company share value, at least in the USA, is the price-earnings ratio (P/E ratio). This ratio represents the current price per share to earnings per share (EPS). P/E ratios are published in the financial press daily. If, for example, the closing stock price P = $100 and annual EPS is $10, then the P/E multiple = $100/$10 = 10. The P/E can be interpreted to mean that if it is 10, investors pay $10 per share per $1 of current earnings. Likewise, if the P/E is 8, investors pay $8 per $1 of current earnings. Assuming two companies are similar in all respects, investors would choose the company with the lower P/E as they would be acquiring a claim on a dollar of earnings more cheaply.

The reciprocal of the P/E ratio, or E/P, is measured as earnings per share divided by the current stock price, and is a percentage figure that evaluates the investment's profitability. The E/P is called the earnings yield. The earnings yield normally should be higher than the dividend payout ratio. If the payout ratio is higher than the earnings yield, than the company is paying dividends from its reserves or from an increase in debt. If such a situation occurs for more than one year, the company will probably decrease its dividend payments.

One limitation of the P/E or E/P ratios is that they are based on the past year's earnings. In actuality, investors are concerned with future earnings and dividends and not with past earnings. However, the E/P ratio exhibits a measure of profitability that is equal to the one implied by the constant dividend growth model when the following are true of a company:

1 It has constant earnings, when all earnings are distributed as cash dividends
2 There is constant growth in earnings and dividends as long as the firm has a normal growth rate and pays annual dividends as a fixed percentage of its earnings.

Stocks with high P/E ratios are usually labelled as growth stocks. When two companies are compared that have the same current earnings per share, but one is a high-growth company and the other a low-growth company, the high-growth company should have the higher share price and thus a higher P/E ratio. In general, firms that are expected to have higher earnings growth will have higher P/E ratios and are thus known as growth stocks.

On the other hand, stocks with low P/E ratios are referred to as value stocks. Low P/E stocks are often viewed as inexpensive to current earnings. They may represent good investment value in the future, and thus are known as value stocks.

It is the variation in expected growth rates that causes differences in P/E rates amongst firms. The P/E ratio reflects the market's optimism concerning a company's growth projections. An analyst or fund manager who is more optimistic than the market will recommend buying the stock; if the opposite holds true, the analyst should recommend selling the stock.

Another limitation to P/E analysis is that the earnings portion of the ratio is affected by certain accounting rules, such as the use of historical cost for depreciation. If inflation happens to be unusually high, historic cost depreciation will tend to under-represent true economic values because the replacement cost of the goods will rise with the general level of prices. P/E ratios have tended to be lower when inflation has been higher. Also, besides having different accounting policies, different countries have different tax policies, which will also affect the earnings component of the P/E ratio – making it difficult to compare companies in different countries. Other ratios, such as EV/EBITDA (where EV = Enterprise value = Market capitalization + Net debt – Estimated value of 'non-core' Assets, and EBITDA = Earnings before interest tax, depreciation, and amortization), may be more appropriate for company valuation comparisons in cases where companies are being compared across sectors in different countries.

Again, P/E ratios are most often used by analysts and fund managers in conjunction with other valuation measures, or at least with other price ratio figures, in order to assess investment opportunities.

Price to sales ratio

Another ratio that financial analysts use to assess a firm's performance is the price to sales (P/S) ratio. This ratio is calculated by taking the company's current stock price and dividing that by the company's current or most recent annual sales revenue per share figure:

$$\frac{P}{S} = \frac{\text{Share price}}{\text{Annual sales revenue per share}}$$

This ratio determines a company's ability to engender sales growth. A high P/S ratio implies that the company has high sales growth; a low P/S multiple indicates slow sales growth. Often, the multiple of one company is compared to similar companies within the same sector to determine how the company is doing versus its peers. If a company's P/S ratio is similar to that of an industry average, then the expectation is that the company's revenue might only be expected to grow at the same rate as the industry median.

Price to book ratio

Price to book ratio (P/B) is another ratio sometimes utilized by analysts and fund managers. P/B equals the market value of the firm's outstanding common stock divided by the book value of the equity. Book value essentially equals a company's assets minus its liabilities. It represents the amount of capital invested in a company through retained earnings and through stock issuance.

$$\frac{P}{BV} = \frac{\text{Share price}}{\text{Book value per share}}$$

The ratio measures what the equity is worth today (share price) versus what it cost (book value). A ratio larger than 1.0 indicates that a firm has successfully created value for its shareholders. A ratio of less than 1.0 shows that a company is trading at less than it cost. Investors searching for value stocks may look for companies whose share prices are near or below their book value.

Price to book does have some limitations. Accounting standards have changed over time, and asset values may not have been adjusted properly for inflation. Book values may thus become distorted, and difficulties may arise when comparing book values across sectors or countries. Nonetheless, the price to book ratio is often used when analysing values in the banking sector. Price to book ratios are often compared to return on equity figures. Thus if two banks have the same price to book but one bank has a greater ROE, the bank with the greater ROE would appear to be a more appealing investment.

Price to cash flow ratio

The price to cash flow ratio (P/CF) is yet another type of price ratio employed by analysts and fund managers in their quest to assess company value properly. P/CF equals the firm's current stock price divided by its current annual cash flow per share:

$$\frac{P}{CF} = \frac{\text{Share price}}{\text{Annual cash flow per share}}$$

where:

Cash flow = net income plus depreciation
Net income = revenues − expenses.

(There are several ways to calculate cash flow, including the method to calculate free cash flow described previously. For the P/CF ratio here, cash flow is calculated as net income plus depreciation.)

Price to earnings ratios and price to cash flow ratios can be compared to each other. When a firm's earnings per share is not very much higher than its cash flow per share, this points to good quality earnings – i.e. that the accounting earnings reflect the actual cash flow. When the opposite holds true, namely when the value of the earnings and the value of the cash flow diverge from each other, this may indicate poor quality earnings. In the end, analysts like to monitor the trend in the cash flow of a company undiluted by accounting tactics. The price to cash flow ratio is a useful tool with which to monitor and compare a company's value.

Calculating expected future share prices using price ratios

Price ratios can be utilized to estimate future share prices. One way of doing this is to take a historical five-year average price ratio and multiply it by an expected future value for the price ratio denominator value.

For example, Table 8.2 below gives some information on Share X.

Table 8.2 Price ratios (example)

	P/E	P/S	P/CF
Current value per share	$4.56	$15.50	$5.89
5-year average price ratio	11.6	3.0	8.5
5-year average growth rate	25.20%	15.80%	19.25

With this information, next year's share price can be estimated using each of the ratios as follows:

Using the P/E ratio:
Expected price = Average P/E × Current earnings per share × (1 + Average earnings growth rate)

Therefore,
Expected price $= 11.6 \times \$4.56 \times 1.252 = \$66.23$

Using the P/S ratio:

Expected price $=$ Average P/S $\times$ Current sales per share $\times (1 +$ Average sales growth rate)

Therefore,
Expected price $= 3.0 \times \$15.50 \times 1.158 = \$53.85$

Using the P/CF ratio

Expected price $=$ Average P/CF $\times$ Current cash flow per share $\times (1 +$ Average cash flow growth rate)

Therefore,
Expected price $= 8.5 \times \$5.89 \times 1.1925 = \$59.70$

These three price ratio methods each result in a different expected price. This is because they use different inputs. The described formulas use historical growth rates to predict the future. An expected future growth rate could be used in the formulas instead. It is up to analysts or fund managers to call upon their experience to determine the appropriate inputs and estimates. The figures should, however, be in the same ballpark, and will give some indication of future price. However, if the current price of Share X is higher than the expected price, then the conclusion would be that the share is currently overvalued. What is important is that analysts or fund managers are consistent in their method of estimates of future values.

Quiz: Chapter 8

1 Suppose that a stock pays four annual dividends of $50 per year and that the discount rate (k) = 10%. Using the simple dividend discount model, what is the present value of the stock?

   (A) $125
   (B) $159
   (C) $85
   (D) $190
   (E) $65

2 Assuming that a company has a dividend growth rate of 5%, the discount rate is 8%, there are 15 years of annual dividends to be paid and the current dividend is 80p, what is the value of the company's stock, based on the constant dividend growth rate model?

   (A) 80p
   (B) 856p
   (C) 200p
   (D) 965p
   (E) 97p

3 If a company's dividends are projected to grow at 3% in perpetuity, the discount rate is 10%, and the current dividend is $15, what is the value of the stock, using the constant perpetual growth model?

   (A) $23
   (B) $300
   (C) $456
   (D) $54
   (E) $225

4 A company has an ROE of 10%, an EPS of $3.00, and a dividend per share D_0 of $2.48. The discount rate is 7.00% and the current share price is $75. The value of the company's stock is _____ and it is considered to be _____.

(Calculate the retention ratio and the sustainable growth rate and use the perpetual growth model.)

(A) $112, undervalued
(B) $48, undervalued
(C) $48, overvalued
(D) $112, overvalued

5 Consider that a company has a current dividend of $4, and that dividends are expected to grow at the rate of $g_1 = 6\%$ for $t = 5$ years and thereafter grow at the rate of $g_2 = 3\%$. With a discount rate of $k = 9\%$, what is the value of the stock?

(A) $78.13
(B) $58.64
(C) $112.50
(D) $99.78
(E) $48.34

6 The idea behind the _____ approach of valuing stocks is that the intrinsic value of the equity in a firm is equal to the present value of the net cash flows to shareholders that can be created by the company's existing asset base plus the net present value of investments that will be made in the future.

(A) two-stage dividend growth model
(B) constant perpetual growth model
(C) free cash flow model
(D) constant dividend growth rate model
(E) retention ratio model

7 Using the following information on Share Z, what is the estimate of Share Z's next year share price as given by the P/E and by P/CF?

	P/E	P/S	P/CF
Current value per share	$5.50	$14.90	$6.8
5-year average price ratio	10.2	4.0	7.6
5-year average growth rate	15.0%	12.70%	13.0%

(A) $67.17, $58.40
(B) $58.40, $64.52
(C) $64.52, $67.17
(D) $64.52, $58.40
(E) $58.40, $67.17

Chapter 9

Financial statement analysis and financial ratios

Understanding a company's financial statements is an essential step for successful stock selection. Financial statements reveal the details of a company's operating and financial historical performance. Financial authorities require timely dissemination of company financial statements to the public, and investment analysts and fund managers use the data in financial statements to identify problems or opportunities that might affect existing or potential investments. Reported accounting data can be used for comparing similar companies within an industry. The data is also utilized to assess a company's ability to meet financial obligations such as interest payments and subsequently to determine bankruptcy risk. Analysts use accounting data to predict future profitability of companies and to estimate future rates of return in the stock market.

A public company's annual report is a good primary source of company financial information. Other sources such as specialized web sites are also available, for example www.hoovers.com, and the SEC's Electronic Data Gathering and Retrieval archives (EDGAR) accessible at www.sec.gov. In some countries, such as the US, the annual report is updated quarterly; in others, reports are provided semi-annually. The formats and items listed on the reports can also vary from country to country

The financial statement comprises the following three major financial reports:

1 **The income statement** (also known as the profit and loss statement) reports the company's operating performance over the accounting period, and summarizes the company's turnover and expenses
2 **The balance sheet** provides a 'snapshot' of the firm's assets and liabilities on a given date
3 **The cash flow statement** (or statement of sources and uses of funds) reports how the firm generated cash and where it was utilized over the accounting period.

Understanding the format and content of the above reporting statements is crucial in order for analysts and fund managers to provide value-added earnings and cash flow analysis. Accounting data are also useful in assessing the economic prospects of the firm. Economic data used for valuation purposes are based on available accounting data.

The three parts of the financial statement are discussed here in more detail, along with a description of some of the more popular financial ratios used to investigate the sources of a firm's profitability and to evaluate the soundness of the earnings.

The income statement

The income statement shows the profitability of the firm over a period of time, such as a year or a quarter. It summarizes the flow of sales, expenses and earnings during the designated period. The income statement is also known as the profit and loss account, or P&L. It states revenues generated during the operating period, the expenses incurred during that same period, and the firm's net earnings or profits (the difference between revenues and expenses). The income statement helps investors to assess the ability of management to produce profits and to control expenses.

Regarding expenses, four broad classes of expenses are considered:

1 **Cost of good sold:** the direct cost attributable to producing the product sold by the firm

2 **General administrative expenses:** the overhead expenses, including salaries, advertising and other costs that are not directly related to production
3 **Interest expenses:** interest paid on the firm's debt
4 **Taxes on earnings:** taxes owed to federal and local governments.

The information contained in the income statement assists investors in answering numerous questions they may have about the company's profitability. First and foremost, did the company make a profit or a loss? What has the trend in the revenues, costs and profit been over the last few years? What were the primary sources of expenses?

Table 9.1 is a sample income statement for Company Z.

In this case, the company's gross profits and net income have both gone up over the past year. Even though all expenses were up apart from taxes paid, the company experienced an extraordinary loss last year, which reduced net

Table 9.1   Income statement for Company Z (in millions $)

	This year	*Last year*
Net Sales	100	90
Costs of goods sold	(30)	(25)
Gross profit	70	65
Administrative expenses	(10)	(8)
Operating income	60	57
Investment income	5	5
Interest expense	(3)	(1)
Income before tax	62	61
Income taxes	(14)	(14)
Minority interest income	1	1
Profit after tax	49	48
Extraordinary items	0	(2)
Net income	**49**	**46**
Dividends	(12)	(11)
Retained earnings	37	35

income. Dividends were also slightly higher this year due to the higher net income. Net income is often the last line of the income statement. In this example, however, dividends and retained earnings information have been added. One point of note is that the sum of dividends and retained earnings is equal to net income:

Net income = Dividends + Retained earnings

Operating income is the difference between operating revenues and operating costs. Income from other sources is then added to obtain earnings before interest and taxes (EBIT). This is what the firm would have earned if it were not for obligations to its creditors and tax authorities. In this case, EBIT would equal 65 (operating income of 60 plus investment income of 5) for this year.

One major expense that requires close observation is depreciation. The way an asset changes in value over time can be markedly different from how it is expensed on the income statement. Also, firms can depreciate assets using different methods, and inflation can distort the difference between an asset's economic value and accounting value. A firm's EBITDA is equal to earnings before interest, tax, depreciation and amortization.

The balance sheet

The balance sheet enumerates the assets, liabilities, and equity of a firm on a given date. The balance sheet is based on the following identity equation:

Assets = Liabilities + Owners' equity

Another way of putting this equation is that the difference in assets and liabilities is the net worth of the firm, or the stockholders' (owners') equity. The balance sheet determines the size of the firm, the balance between fixed and current assets, and the firm's capital structure.

The first part of the balance sheet shows a listing of the assets of the firm, starting with current assets. Current assets are cash items or items that can be easily converted to cash, or items that will be used within a year. For example, accounts receivable will be collected as cash, and inventory will be sold. Next on the balance sheet comes a listing of long-term assets or fixed assets, which have an expected life of more than one year and are used in normal business operations. Fixed assets may be tangible or intangible. Tangible assets include property, plants and equipment, while intangible assets include patents and licences. Except for land, fixed assets normally depreciate in value over time. Securities held for investment purposes are also considered to be long-term assets.

The liability and stockholders' equity (also called shareholders' equity) section of the balance sheet starts with the short-term or current liabilities, which include accounts payable, accrued taxes, and debts that are due within one year. Next are the long-term debt and other longer-term liabilities that are due in more than a year. Other liabilities include assorted items that do not belong to any other liability category. Stockholders' equity is the difference between total assets and total liabilities. This represents the net worth or book value of the firm. Stockholders' equity is broken down into paid-in capital, which is the proceeds realized from the sale of stock to the public, and retained earnings, which are accumulated earnings not paid out as dividends and used to finance company growth. Even if a firm issues no new equity, the book value should increase each year as long as retained earnings of the firm are increasing.

Table 9.2 is a sample balance sheet for Company Z.

In Table 9.2, the main changes to the balance sheet are an increase in property and plant due to a purchase of some new land, an increase in long-term debt due to an issuance of a new bond, and changes to the depreciation amount and cash.

Also, as can be seen from the above example, the total assets equal the total liabilities plus shareholders' equity. It is extremely important to read the 'Notes to the Financial Statements' section, which accompanies the financial reports. Here will be found the accounting conventions used to calculate how inventories, raw materials, work in progress and finished goods are carried on the balance sheet, and the depreciation policy applied

Table 9.2 Balance sheet for Company Z (in millions $)

	This year	Last year
Assets		
Cash	60	33
Accounts receivable	100	100
Inventories	400	400
Other current assets	200	200
Total current assets	760	733
Property and plant	800	620
Equipment	200	200
Accumulated depreciation	(100)	(30)
Other investments	50	50
Intangibles	10	10
Other assets	20	20
Total assets	**1740**	**1603**
Liabilities		
Short-term debt	100	100
Accounts payable	40	40
Other current liabilities	150	150
Total current liabilities	290	290
Long-term debt	370	270
Minority interest	10	10
Other liabilities	200	200
Total Liabilities	**870**	**770**
Paid-in capital	300	300
Retained earnings	570	533
Total shareholders' equity	870	833
Total liabilities and shareholders' equity	**1740**	**1603**

to property, plant and equipment. Different conventions apply to different industries and in different countries.

The cash flow statement

The cash flow statement reports the company's sources and uses of cash over a specific period. It reports the cash flow generated by the company's operations, investments, and financial activities. The statement of cash flows recognizes only transactions where actual cash is involved. For example, if the company sells a product now but payment is only due in 60 days, the income statement and the balance sheet will immediately be adjusted by the sales amount, whereas the cash flow statement will not recognize the transaction until the bill is paid and cash is in hand. Cash flow also differs from income in that income contains non-cash items, such as depreciation, which must be added back to net income when calculating cash flow.

Operating cash flow is reported in the first section of the cash flow statement. The second section of the statement is investment cash flow, which includes any purchases or sales of fixed assets and investments. Following that is the financing cash flow section, which includes any funds raised by the issuance of new securities or funds used to repurchase outstanding securities. Dividend payments are considered financing cash flows, whereas interest payments are considered operating cash flows. The sum of the operating cash flow, investment cash flow, and financing cash flow produces the net change in the company's cash level. This figure reveals how much cash flowed into or out of the firm's cash account during an accounting period.

Table 9.3 is a simplified sample statement of cash flow for Company Z:

Table 9.3 Statement of cash flow for Company Z (in millions of $)

	This year
Net income	49
Depreciation	100
Operating cash flow	149
Investment cash flow	(180)
Financing cash flow	88
Net cash Increase	57

In the example, the net income is adjusted by adding back depreciation. The investment cash flow amount is due to the purchase of some land (property and plant). Long-term debt increased by $100 m, but is adjusted by the $12 m dividend payout to attain the $88 m financing cash flow figure.

Ratio analysis

Ratio analysis is used to compare the financial trends of a company over a given time horizon. Ratio analysis facilitates the comparison of firms of different sizes, and it helps to identify the risks as well as potential earnings growth inherent to a given company. Ratios are typically categorized into three groups: liquidity ratios, profitability ratios and leverage ratios. Liquidity ratios measure the ability of the firm to pay its immediate liabilities; profitability ratios measure the firm's earning potential; and leverage or debt ratios indicate the financial risk of a firm by evaluating the firm's ability to pay its debt obligations. Below is a summary of some key financial ratios.

Liquidity ratios

$$\text{Current ratio} = \frac{\text{Current assets}}{\text{Current liabilities}}$$

The current ratio shows to what extent the claims of short-term creditors are covered by assets which can be converted to cash in a short time frame.

$$\text{Quick ratio (acid test ratio)} = \frac{\text{Current assets} - \text{Inventory}}{\text{Current liabilities}}$$

This ratio measures the firm's ability to pay off short-term obligations without relying on the sale of its inventories

Profitability ratios

$$\text{Gross profit margin} = \frac{\text{Sales} - \text{Cost of goods sold}}{\text{Sales}}$$

The gross profit margin indicates the total margin available to cover operating expenses and still yield a profit.

$$\text{Operating profit margin (return on sales)} = \frac{\text{Profits before taxes and interest}}{\text{Sales}}$$

The operating profit margin shows the firm's profitability from current operations without taking into consideration the interest charges.

$$\text{Net profit margin (net return on sales)} = \frac{\text{Profits after taxes}}{\text{Sales}}$$

This ratio measures the after tax profits per unit of sales. Low profit margins indicate that the firm's sales prices are relatively low or that its costs are relatively high, or both.

$$\text{Return on stockholder's equity} = \frac{\text{Profits after taxes}}{\text{Total stockholders' equity}}$$

The return on stockholders' equity or return on net worth, as the ratio is also sometimes called, shows the rate of return on stockholders' investment in the company.

Leverage ratios

$$\text{Debt to asset ratio} = \frac{\text{Total debt}}{\text{Total assets}}$$

This ratio measures the extent to which borrowed funds have been utilized to finance the company's operations

$$\text{Debt to equity ratio} = \frac{\text{Total debt}}{\text{Total stockholders' equity}}$$

The debt to equity ratio provides a comparative measure of the funds provided by creditors versus the funds provided by owners.

$$\text{Interest cover ratio} = \frac{\text{Profits before interest and taxes}}{\text{Total interest charges}}$$

This ratio measures how easily the company can meet its interest obligations.

Other ratios

$$\text{Dividend payout ratio} = \frac{\text{Annual dividends per share}}{\text{After tax earnings per share}}$$

The dividend payout ratio indicates the percentage of profits paid out as dividends.

$$\text{Dividend yield on common stock} = \frac{\text{Annual dividends per share}}{\text{Share price}}$$

This ratio provides a measure of the return to the owners received in the form of dividends.

In the previous chapter, price ratios were discussed to analyse stock values. A review of the formulas is given below:

$$\text{Price to earnings ratio} = \frac{\text{Share price}}{\text{After tax earnings per share}}$$

$$\text{Price to book ratio} = \frac{\text{Stock price}}{\text{Book value per share}}$$

$$\text{Price to sales ratio} = \frac{\text{Stock price}}{\text{Annual sales revenue per share}}$$

$$\text{Price to cash flow ratio} = \frac{\text{Share price}}{\text{Annual operating cash flow per share}}$$

Earnings per share

$$\text{Earnings per share} = \frac{\text{Profits after taxes}}{\text{No. of shares of common stock outstanding}}$$

Reported earnings per share (EPS) measures the past performance of the firm. Analysts rely on EPS to form valuation estimates. They usually use the income statement and reported EPS to estimate the future earnings capability of a firm. However, several adjustments must usually be made, including the exclusion in the EPS figure of non-recurring items, such as the one-time sale of an asset.

Analysts will also attempt to assess the quality of the earnings by seeing how much the actual operating earnings differ form reported EPS. Ranking systems are sometimes devised to evaluate the quality of earnings. Low quality implies that the reported EPS number differs significantly form the firm's actual operating earnings. An analyst will seek to analyse how stable the earnings are over time, and whether the accounting procedures employed by the company are conservative or liberal. Other checks on quality of earnings include monitoring accounts receivables for large increases, checking for many one-time sources of income, and reading the independent auditor's report. If auditors have reservations about the financial statements of a company, they will usually express these in the letter to shareholders and Board of Directors. However, as a point of note, auditors do not always discover problems with the accounts.

Examples

Using the financial statements given above for Company Z, some financial ratios can be calculated for this year as follows:

$$\text{Acid test ratio} = \frac{\text{Current assets} - \text{Inventory}}{\text{Current liabilities}}$$

$$= \frac{760 - 400}{290}$$

$$= 1.24$$

$$\text{Net profit margin} = \frac{\text{Profit after taxes}}{\text{Sales}}$$

$$= \frac{49}{100}$$

$$= 49\%$$

$$\text{Debt to equity ratio} = \frac{\text{Total debt}}{\text{Total stockholders' equity}}$$

$$= \frac{(100 + 370)}{870}$$

$$= 54\%$$

$$\text{Interest cover} = \frac{\text{Profit before interest and taxes}}{\text{Total interest charges}}$$

$$= \frac{65}{3}$$

$$= 21.7$$

The sampling of ratios above shows that Company Z is in a relatively comfortable position. Its net profit margins are quite high at 49%, and even though the debt to equity ratio is high at over 50%, the interest cover is extremely good with profits covering interest charges over 21 times. The acid test ratio shows that the current assets minus inventory can more than cover the current liabilities.

Assuming the number of shares outstanding for Company Z is 35 million both this year and last year, and that the year-end stock price this year is $20, the following ratios can also be calculated:

$$\text{EPS (this year)} = \frac{\text{Profits after taxes}}{\text{No. of shares of common stock outstanding}}$$

$$= \frac{\$49}{35}$$

$$= \$1.40$$

$$\text{EPS (last year)} = \frac{\$46}{35}$$

$$= \$1.31$$

$$\text{EPS growth rate} = \frac{\$1.40 - \$1.31}{\$1.31}$$

$$= \$6.9\%$$

$$\text{P/E ratio} = \frac{\text{Share price}}{\text{After tax earnings per share}}$$

$$= \frac{\$20}{\$1.40}$$

$$= 14.3$$

The P/E ratio is not particularly high at 14.3, but given an EPS growth rate of about 7%, a high P/E ratio would not be expected. Whether a 7% EPS growth rate would be considered low depends on the economic environment in place at the time. If the economy is in a recession, a 7% growth rate might look attractive. A comparison of actual and expected EPS growth rate of similar companies in the same sector would also point to whether Company Z's EPS growth rate was considered low, average, or even high. A similar comparative analysis would also be done for the company's P/E ratio.

The interpretation of financial ratios is a skill that takes practice. Different analysts in different countries can utilize slightly different methods of calculating ratios. Also, analysts must become particularly astute at monitoring accounts for techniques of creative accounting or financial engineering. Analysts often back up their study of the company accounts by visits to the companies themselves to 'kick the tyres' and verify information that is presented in the financial statements.

Quiz: Chapter 9

1   A company's overhead costs including salaries and advertising are known as _____ and are found in the _____ .

   (A)   cost of goods sold, income statement
   (B)   general administrative expenses, income statement
   (C)   interest expenses, income statement
   (D)   general administrative expenses, balance sheet
   (E)   cost of goods sold, balance sheet

2   Using the financial statement information for Company Z, what is the company's current ratio for this year?

   (A)   2.62
   (B)   1.24
   (C)   2.00
   (D)   0.50
   (E)   0.40

3   Using the financial statement information for Company Z, the company's gross profit margin for this year and for last year are _____ and _____ .

   (A)   49%, 51%
   (B)   62%, 68%
   (C)   60%, 63%
   (D)   37%, 39%
   (E)   70%, 72%

4   What is the rate of return on stockholders' investment in Company Z this year, using the data given in the chapter?

   (A)   8.6%
   (B)   2.8%
   (C)   5.6%
   (D)   16.8%
   (E)   15.4%

5 Company Z's dividend payout ratios for this year and for last year
   are _____ and _____ .

   (A) 24.5%, 23.9%
   (B) 19.4%, 18.0%
   (C) 20.0%, 19.3%
   (D) 32.4%, 31.4%
   (E) 17.1%, 16.9%

6 Consider two stocks. Stock X has a P/E ratio of 15, an EPS of 6.7%
   and an earnings growth rate of 10%; stock Y has a P/E ratio of 20,
   an EPS of 5% and an earnings growth rate of 20%. The share prices
   of both stocks are 100. In a year's time, stock X's share price will be
   _____ and stock Y's share price will be _____ .
   The better investment will be _____ .

   (A) 111, 120, stock X
   (B) 115, 125, stock Y
   (C) 115, 125, stock X
   (D) 111, 120, stock Y
   (E) 100, 120, stock Y

Chapter 10

Types of funds explained

Investors now have more of a choice than ever in choosing which types of funds suit their investment and risk needs. This chapter looks at some of issues relating to the more popular types of funds available, ranging from the passive to the most active.

Tracker funds

Index tracking (or indexing) is a version of the buy and hold strategy that eliminates diversifiable risk. This type of fund management attempts to avoid, as much as possible, decisions about stock selection and timing. It is not purely passive, however, as the choice of index and the reinvestment of income are active choices. There is also the chance that the fund will underperform the index and suffer some tracking error, as it is virtually impossible to be exactly indexed at all time. Of course, transaction costs will also eat into the performance figures.

Considerable latitude of both strategic and tactical decision-making remains with the investor since he or she will be choosing from a comprehensive mix of indices, ranging from broad indices to sub-indices, in order to meet risk and return goals. The indices chosen can also comply with portfolio constraints such as avoiding the securities of companies dealing with tobacco or alcohol. Tracker funds can be formulated for equity and/or bond investments.

From the point of view of managing an index fund, the approach is systems intensive. Indexing is basically a quantitative approach to fund management, and specific hardware and software systems are essential for the management of these funds. Special computer programming is needed to process pricing and trading information, to calculate market capitalization weightings, to make comparisons with the theoretical benchmarks and to determine the trades necessary to adjust the real portfolio. In addition the fund manager must track a further array of information, including dividend payments, mergers and acquisitions, stock splits, bonus and rights issues, index changes, commissions, and taxes.

Since tracker funds basically hold the market, or the index selected to represent a particular market, the number of securities held tends to be substantially greater than those in an actively managed portfolio. Also, a well-constructed index fund will tend to incur fewer trades compared to an active portfolio. The largest source of trading costs in an index fund is the reinvestment of dividends. Also, annual turnover of securities in a tracker fund is much lower than in an active fund where the turnover figure can reach 100% or more. Thus, tracker funds can be considered more tax efficient. Index fund managers tend to pay less in broker commission as they transact on an execution-only basis, and costs for tracker funds can range from a little over 0.50% for small cap indexed funds to below 0.20% for large-cap indexed funds. Active fund managers will tend to transact on a research plus cost basis.

Besides tracking the index, another concern of the portfolio manager is the need to rebalance the fund periodically. The addition and deletion of securities that constitute the index, the collection of dividends, and the infusion of new contributions all cause the composition of the fund to deviate from the index. If the portfolio manager fails to compensate for these changes, the tracker fund risks not being able to match the returns of the index. In dealing with rebalancing, the index manager can chose either to replicate or to sample. Full replication means buying every security in the index in the amount matching the exact weighting in the index, whereas sampling involves purchasing a smaller amount of securities that will approximate the same characteristics (i.e. yield, industry sector and company size) and returns of the index. Sampling may result in lower transaction costs, but these funds may not provide the same returns as a fully replicated fund. (Since the tracking error for a fund using sampling will be higher, the fund may underperform or outperform the index more than a replicated fund does.)

Over the last several decades tracker funds have grown in popularity worldwide, especially after periods of time when actively managed funds underperformed their indices. Investors will continue to be attracted by indexing's features in terms of cost, return, risk, liquidity and diversification.

Exchange traded funds

Exchange traded funds (ETFs) are basically index funds that are listed on exchanges, and trade like stocks. ETFs are designed to track sector or country indices. The rise and fall in the value of these indices is expressed in terms of single shares. Investors can, by purchasing the shares, buy the precise amounts of the index they want to track. ETFs enable investors to gain broad exposure to entire stock markets in different countries and to specific sectors on a real-time basis, and at a lower cost than many other forms of investing. They are bought on a commission basis, and can be purchased on margin. Also, ETFs can be used to short indices. The annual expenses range from 0.09% to 0.99%, and are deducted from dividend payments typically paid twice a year. ETFs are priced continuously throughout the day, and their components are disclosed every trading day.

Some of the most popular ETFs include:

■ SPDRs: depositary receipts mimicking the S&P 500 index
■ iShares: numerous funds tracking different US and foreign indices
■ DIAMONDS: track the Dow Jones Industrial Average
■ QQQ: track the Nasdaq composite index.

Many ETFs have been created to track every type of equity index, including the stock markets of individual countries, industrial sectors and smaller-sized companies. Fixed income (bond) ETFs now also exist. Both institutional and retail investors can invest in ETFs.

A key feature that distinguishes ETFs is that creating and redeeming shares occurs outside the normal stock exchange transaction process, thus avoiding trading costs. When demand for an ETF is expected, a large intermediary broker/dealer or authorized participant (AP) buys securities representing an underlying index. The value of the portfolio is calculated at the close of that trading day, and the basket of stocks is then delivered to a custodian bank. In addition, a cash component is delivered to the custodian to cover fees associated with the creation, as well as accrued dividends, interest on dividends, and any capital gains less losses on the basket of stocks that have not been reinvested since the last distribution. At settlement, the custodian bank gives the AP ETF shares (usually in blocks of 50 000 shares). The ETF shares trade without restraint between investors.

The ETF portfolio net asset value (NAV) is calculated at the close of each trading day. When investors decide to exit an ETF, the ETF shares are delivered to the custodian. At settlement, the securities comprising the underlying index plus a cash component are delivered to the AP. Nominal transaction fees are deducted.

ETFs are created in block-sized 'creation units', and can only be redeemed in redemption units or 'in-kind' for a portfolio of stocks held in by the fund. The key characteristic of 'in-kind' distribution of securities is that it does not create a tax event, which would otherwise occur if the fund sold securities and delivered cash.

Some of the investment applications and investment concerns relating to ETFs as determined by ETF expert Deborah A. Fuhr at Morgan Stanley are listed below:

Investment applications

- ETFs can be a good alternative to futures for managing cash flows, as they can be bought in smaller sizes than futures and are available on benchmarks for which there are no futures contracts.
- ETFs can be used to implement sector rotation and sector allocation strategies and to adjust sector or country exposure.
- ETFs can be used to hedge sector, country or regional exposure, as they can be sold short.

- Index-linked ETFs' expense ratios are lower than those of traditional mutual funds or unit trusts.
- Broad-based ETFs can be used as diversified core holdings, while sector ETFs can be used to complete parts of portfolios for tactical strategies.
- Index-linked ETFs generally have a tax advantage over open-ended US-based mutual funds because redemptions do not force a sale of stocks and thus a taxable event.

Investment concerns

- ETFs carry the risks applicable to index funds, including general risks of investing in securities and the risk that an index-linked fund might underperform a more actively traded fund.
- Besides the commission an investor pays when buying or selling an ETF, he or she must also be aware of the bid/ask spread (difference between the purchase and sale price) quoted on the ETF. If the ETF is not widely traded, the spread could be wide.
- The closing price of an ETF may be at a premium or discount to its net asset value (NAV). This difference will affect reported performance of the ETF versus the index.
- Index-linked ETFs are exposed to tracking error risk, which leads to an imperfect correlation between an ETF's stocks and those in its underlying index. Factors such as fees and expenses, dividend reinvestments, rebalancing transaction costs, and computer-optimized replication may cause the ETF's return to deviate from that of the underlying index.

Active fund management styles

Within the active fund management segment of portfolio management, fund managers pursue a variety of investment techniques known as styles of investing. Two of the more popular styles are growth stock investing and value stock investing (low valuation stock investing). Another determinant of style is the market capitalization size of a company, thus leading to large-cap and small-cap investment styles. Fund managers will present themselves to clients as, for example, an aggressive growth, an emerging market, or a technology portfolio manager. These categorizations imply that a fund or a manager invests in a distinct group of stocks that have some characteristics in common. These grouping of stocks can be viewed as subcomponents of a broader stock market. Consequently, these sub-components allow the portfolio manager the opportunity to develop strategies based on differing stock group behaviour. In turn, investors are presented with a wider variety of investment choice.

Table 10.1 delineates some of the categories of investment style. Further styles exist related to international regions or specific sectors. Various

Table 10.1 UK domestic style categories

Value	Stocks that trade at low multiples of price to measures of fundamental value. Ratios used to define value strategies include the dividend yield, the price to earnings ratio and the ratio of price to book value per share. Such stocks tend to feature relatively low expected earnings growth. In recent years value stocks have concentrated in established, stable industries such as manufacturing utilities and foods.
Growth	Companies with strong growth expectations. These commonly trade at prices that are high relative to current earnings, dividends or book values.
Momentum	Stocks that have performed very well recently. Usually focuses on periods up to one year. The assumption is that recent good performance will continue. This style has become increasingly popular.
Contrarian	In contrast to the momentum strategy, these stocks have performed badly. However, contrarian strategies commonly look at the performance over several years, whereas momentum strategies usually focus on the past year.
Small-cap	Companies with small market capitalizations. The Hoare Govett Smaller Companies Index, for example, targets the bottom tenth of the UK market by aggregate market value.
Micro-cap	Stocks with extremely small market capitalizations. The ABN AMRO/LBS MicroCap Index, for example, covers UK companies that represent the bottom 1% by aggregate market value.
Large-cap	The biggest companies, also known as blue chips. Whereas small-cap and micro-cap investors hope for relatively good performance from small companies, large-cap investors prefer safety.

Source: Elroy Dimson and Stefan Nagel (2001) Seeking out investment value in styles. *FT/Mastering Investment*, Part One, 14 May.

combinations are possible, such as eurozone value and mid-cap growth. One style that is gaining popularity is 'GARP' or growth at a reasonable price.

The role of investment consultants may have influenced the importance of investment styles. Their job is to assess fund managers' skills on behalf of their clients. In order to measure a portfolio manager's performance accurately, the consultant will want to assess the skill in selecting stocks compared to the performance of the style a manager follows. Hence, style-based performance measurement and style-based benchmarks are now common. Many style indices have been developed to monitor style-based market segments.

Different styles tend to come in and out of favour. In recent history, high-growth styles (e.g. Internet company funds) did very well at the expense of the value style. Certain value-based funds were doing so poorly that they were actually forced to shut down. This trend then reversed, and the high-growth funds saw large downward corrections whilst the value-type funds came more into favour. Investors may choose to diversify their investments by investing in portfolios that offer different styles. Also, portfolio managers and investors may rotate styles and change the weighting placed in different themes over time. (Generally portfolio managers gain their reputation as experts in a particular style, and it is often difficult for them to change from one style to another.)

Style rotation is thus based on the notion that returns on particular styles may be predictable. A model for forecasting style returns is needed to implement style rotation. This model will include a variety of variables such as macroeconomic indicators, recent style performance, measures of the spread in valuation ratios between styles, and measures of investor sentiment. With such a model, an investor may be able to enhance returns by switching from one style to another over time.

If a fund manager does implement a style rotational strategy in a portfolio, he or she will need to earn the transactions costs that will be incurred. Rotation involves a higher turnover of the portfolio and, consequently, higher transaction costs.

Peer group comparison (comparing managers with a peer group that follows a similar style with similar portfolio constraints) has become a common way to evaluate fund manager performance. It is also possible to estimate how much of a manager's performance is due to style exposure and how much is due to stock selection. Investment consultants run detailed performance attribution models to evaluate different fund managers' skills for their clients.

Overall, identifying and marketing their portfolio management style has become essential for fund management companies in order to win fund management mandates. Many money management companies offer a variety of styles and leave it up to clients to choose or allocate amongst the styles they think will outperform or that best suits their needs.

Alternative investments

Hedge funds, private equity, and managed futures all come under the category of alternative investments, along with investments in collectable objects such as artwork and fine wine. Increasingly, large investors such as pension funds are beginning to add alternative investments as a core-satellite strategy, where the core of their investments are made in traditional products such as equity and bond mutual funds, and the satellite or smaller portion of their investments are put into alternative investments such as hedge funds and private equity. Sometimes alternative investing is called absolute return investing, as the object is to target an absolute return range and not returns relative to a predetermined index.

Hedge funds are the most popular category of alternative investment, and are here discussed in more detail, along with some discussion of private equity.

Hedge funds

Hedge funds are a subset of alternative investments, and fall into the category of most actively traded funds. Where traditional funds are measured against a benchmark and are aiming to produce similar or relatively higher returns compared to the benchmark, a hedge fund's goal is to produce absolute returns, adjusted to bear the lowest risk possible for that target return. Hedge funds can take long and short positions, and use futures, options, gearing and other strategies to control the level of potential gains and losses and to minimize the volatility of the portfolio. Because hedge funds can incorporate short positions in the portfolio, they can often produce positive returns in times of market downturns.

Also, hedge fund managers are paid differently from conventional fund managers. Since running a hedge fund is considered more demanding than seeking only relative returns, the hedge fund managers are often rewarded by high fees linked to performance. For example, a manager who performs well and beats a specific absolute return target can earn up to 25% of that gain over and above the annual management fee, which can be between 1% and 2%. On the other hand if there is no absolute return, such managers earn no performance-related fee. The hedge fund manager usually has a significant personal stake in the fund.

Because hedge funds are more sophisticated in the usage of financial techniques and instruments than are traditional unit and investment trusts, they tend to be based in tax-free regions where financial regulation allows greater freedom. The exception is the large number of US domestic hedge funds, where the US Securities and Exchange Commission allows 'accredited and qualified investors' to invest. To qualify as accredited, the individual investor must have a net worth of over $1 million (excluding home and automobile) or two years of an annual income of $200 000 or more with the reasonable expectation that this income level will continue into the future. A qualified purchaser must have a $5 million investment portfolio. Qualified institutional investors, such as pension funds, must have capital of at least $25 million. Some hedge funds require that investors be both qualified and accredited. Wealthy individuals form the largest group of investors in hedge funds. In the UK, hedge funds are not allowed to market to retail investors, but as long as a client can fund the minimum investment, he or she can invest in the hedge fund. Regulations in the hedge fund realm are evolving with a bent towards further enhanced regulation to make hedge funds available to a wider pool of investors.

While traditional funds are organized around styles that reflect market segments or quantitative characteristics, hedge funds are organized around strategies (see Table 10.2).

Table 10.2 Classification of hedge funds

Non-directional strategies

Fixed income arbitrage	Having long and short bond positions via cash or derivatives markets in government, corporate and/or asset-backed securities. The risk varies with duration, credit exposure and the degree of leverage.
Event-driven	A strategy that hopes to benefit from mispricing arising from different events, such as merger arbitrage or restructuring. Managers take a position in an undervalued security that is anticipated to rise in value because of events such as mergers, reorganizations or takeovers. The main risk is that the predicted event does not happen.
Equity hedge	Investment in equity or equity-like instruments where the net exposure is generally low. The manager may invest globally, or have a more defined geographic, industry or capitalization focus. The risk relates primarily to the risk of specific long and short positions.
Distressed securities	Buying and occasionally shorting securities of companies which have filed for creditor protection under Chapter 11 in the US and/or ones undergoing reorganization. The securities range from senior secured debt to common stock. Liquidation of a financially distressed company is the main source of risk.
Merger arbitrage	Buying the securities of a company that is being acquired and shorting that of the acquiring company. The risk associated with such strategies is more of a 'deal' risk than a market risk.
Convertible arbitrage	Buying and selling different securities of the same issuer (such as convertibles or common stock) and seeking to obtain low volatility returns by arbitraging the relative mispricing of these securities.

Directional strategies

Macro	Seeking to capitalize on country, regional or economic change affecting securities, commodities, interest rates and currency rates. Asset allocation can be aggressive, and leverage and derivatives may be used. The method and degree of hedging can vary significantly.
Emerging markets	A strategy that employs a 'growth' or 'value' approach to investing in equities with no shorting or hedging to minimize inherent market risk. These funds mainly invest in the emerging markets, where there may be restrictions on short sales.
Equity non-hedge	Similar to equity hedging with significant net long-exposure.
Short selling	Selling short over-valued securities, with the hope of buying them back at a lower price.

Source: Vikas Agarwal and Narayan Naik (2001) Creative funds that have come into their own. *FT/Mastering Investment*, Part Five, 11 June.

Non-directional strategies are commonly referred to as 'market neutral' strategies, and do not depend on the direction of any specific market movement. In this strategy, the sum of the short positions equals the sum of the long positions. With sector neutral strategies, the portfolio may have limited systematic or market risk and lower volatility. (Sometimes, however, although a hedge fund may appear to be market neutral, due to liquidity constraints or other factors, the fund will not be completely balanced.) Non-directional strategies aim to exploit short-term market inefficiencies and pricing discrepancies between related securities while hedging as much of the market risk as possible. Directional strategies are designed to take advantage of broad movements in the market.

A hedge fund can use gearing or leverage either explicitly or implicitly. Explicit leverage refers to the fund's ratio of their assets to net worth, which can be seen from the balance sheet. Implicit leverage alludes to the ability of the hedge fund to leverage the portfolio by buying securities on margin, or through the use of short positions and derivatives. By employing leverage in the portfolio, the hedge fund can multiply its returns (and risk) on arbitrage opportunities in the market.

Studies regarding the relationship between performance and size of the portfolio show that performance is likely to be negatively related to the size of assets under management. The argument is that there is a limited number of profitable arbitrage opportunities in the market, which make it difficult for hedge funds to invest large sums of money in the medium term. (This size limitation may not be the case for all hedge fund strategies, however.) Consequently, many hedge funds limit their sizes and also impose time restrictions on investments into the fund (e.g. 12 months' minimum time period before money can be withdrawn from the fund). Besides the size of the fund, another risk to the outcome of performance of the fund is manager risk. The skill and experience of the fund manager tends to contribute a significant proportion of overall returns of hedge funds.

In summary, all hedge funds are not necessarily the risky investments that many investors perceive them to be, although they are not open to the general public and are not as closely regulated as more traditional funds. Conservative investment managers whose goals are to produce steady absolute returns with low volatility run many of these funds. Risk can be reduced even further for an investor if he or she invests in a diversified fund of hedge funds, whereby a fund is set up which comprises selected hedge funds. Although risk is diversified, an extra layer of costs is incurred (the fund of funds will charge its fees, and each of the hedge funds within the umbrella fund will charge its own fees).

Private equity

Another subset of the alternative investment realm is private equity. In very general terms, private equity funds invest in securities which are not publicly traded. Types of private equity investment strategies include leveraged buyouts, venture capital investments, distressed debt investments and mezzanine debt investments. Traditionally, private equity is an illiquid investment vehicle. As it is not listed, there is no daily pricing of the product. The time horizon for obtaining returns in private equity investing can be longer than for other funds – private equity funds generally have a ten-year life cycle. Another aspect of private equity is that the fund managers are very active in managing and growing the companies within their funds.

Private equity investing often provides the necessary combination of capital, business mentoring and financial discipline that are essential to fostering private enterprise. Private equity allows for investors to access emerging trends in the economy efficiently. For example, companies such as Microsoft, Amazon.com, Intel and Vodafone were all backed by venture capital private equity.

Stages of funding exist within the scope of venture capital investing. At the earliest stage, seed capital provides the funding for the initial development of the project. Next, start-up financing is provided to companies for use in the product development and marketing in situations where companies have not yet sold their product commercially. Also, there is 'other early-stage' financing that provides companies that have finished the product development phase with further funds to initiate commercial sales. Generally, these companies will not yet be generating a profit. Expansion financing is provided for the growth and expansion of an established company. Secondary purchase financing is the purchase of existing shares in a company from another venture capital firm or another shareholder.

Non-venture-capital private equity investing includes management buy-outs (MBOs), where funds are provided to assist current management teams in acquiring an existing business or product line. Likewise, management buy-ins (MBIs) involve making funds available to an external manager or group of managers to buy into an established company. Private equity investments have played a role in pioneering technological and medical development.

In the US, UK and mainland Europe, most private equity funds take the form of limited partnerships. In these cases, private equity firms act as the general partner responsible for managing the fund and providing vital expertise. Investors in the funds become limited partners, and the returns to all the participants are defined in the partnership agreement. The agreement generally includes an annual management fee to the general partner and a share to the limited partners in the capital gain of the fund once it has reached a threshold return. One limitation of this partnership structure is that there are restricted exit opportunities as there is no secondary market for these investment products. One exit strategy for private equity investors is publicly to list the stock of the company on a stock exchange. The caveat is that economic conditions for the listing may not be ideal at the time when investors want to exit their private equity investments and redeem their investment. Also, there may be little demand for the new shares as many new companies start out as small- or micro-cap companies.

Although private equity has been primarily in the domain of the sophisticated investor, retail investors do have limited opportunities for investing in this investment vehicle. With private equity, the main constraints for many investors involve issues such as illiquidity, length of investment life cycle, costs, and transparency. For unlisted securities the opportunities to buy or sell a position are both complex and expensive, as it may be difficult to establish an accurate price for the investment, let alone assess the risk, volatility, and standard deviation associated with the investment. Thus, private equity can be considered a risky investment for retail investors. However, for long-term institutional investors such vehicles can be an ideal high-risk, high-return investment alternative providing essential portfolio diversification.

Corporate governance

Increasingly, corporate governance issues have moved into the forefront of topics affecting fund management. In recent history, investors have been let down by the complacency surrounding the integrity of financial reporting at companies such as Enron and Worldcom. When companies and their shares collapse, the funds holding the equity can be seriously negatively affected. Thus, globally there is a push to improve and enforce corporate governance at all levels of a commercial activity. The corporate governance movement has focused on auditors, non-executive directors, executive pay, the accuracy of financial statements, and shareholder rights, among other issues.

Corporate governance is the framework through which shareholders are assured legal compliance. In addition, it establishes the appropriate ethical conduct of the corporation. In short, corporate governance is the system of controlling the corporation. The board of directors is the group that exerts corporate control. The board is usually elected by the common shareholders and given specific powers as allowed in the corporate charter and bylaws. The most important job of the board of directors is to appoint the senior management who will carry out the day-to-day affairs of the company. The board also determines the chief executive officer's compensation.

The concentration of shares being held by large institutional investors is rising more and more and the role of active corporate governance by the shareholders is subsequently increasing. For example, if a few large institutional investors get together they can exercise control of a corporation. Risks will increase if these institutional managers use their authority to vote themselves on the board of directors so that they can personally gain. They will not then be acting in the best interest of their clients.

Ideally, good governance policies should ensure that the board develops, executes, and explains policies that focus on reasonable stakeholder concerns, increase shareholder value, lower the cost of capital, and reduce financial, business and operational risk. At the very least, in the US they require company directors to develop controls and processes that enable the board to report on material business and financial risks. In the UK, corporate governance concentrates on the following: that the role of chairman and chief executive be split, that the chairman should not have previously been chief executive, and that non-executives should meet without the chairman or executive directors. The focus on non-executive directors, to ensure that bosses are not mismanaging the companies they run or acting fraudulently, is increasing.

Investors recognize that companies with good corporate governance policies usually command higher market valuations, have cheaper access to capital, and benefit from a stronger shareholder base. There is a trend for companies in less developed markets to implement enhanced corporate governance policies in order to improve their valuations. Increasingly, large money managers are also incorporating corporate governance as an essential criterion in their processes for stock selection. In addition to corporate governance issues, a firm's adherence to best social, ethical, and environmental (SEE) practices is also coming more and more into the forefront of investors' stock selection standards. Legislation relating to corporate governance and SEE is rapidly evolving, and will undoubtedly move these issues into a more important role within the investment process.

Quiz: Chapter 10

1   Usually, in a tracker fund, the largest source of trading costs are
    _____ .

    (A)   stock splits
    (B)   bonus issues
    (C)   mergers and acquisitions
    (D)   dividend reinvestments
    (E)   rights issues

2   If a portfolio manager indexed a portfolio to the sector level, but not
    necessarily to the stock level, this would be known as _____ .

    (A)   value investing
    (B)   sampling
    (C)   hedging
    (D)   replication
    (E)   growth investing

3   _____ involves forecasting returns of different styles in
    order ultimately to enhance returns of the portfolio over time by
    moving from one style to another.

    (A)   Momentum investing
    (B)   Contrarian investing
    (C)   Sampling
    (D)   Replication
    (E)   Style rotation

4   In the US, to be recognized as a qualified investor, an individual
    must have over _____ net worth, and an institutional
    investor must have over _____ in capital.

    (A) $25 million, $5 million
    (B) $10 million, $5 million
    (C) $10 million, $30 million
    (D) $5 million, $25 million
    (E) $5 million, $10 million

5 By employing _____ , a hedge fund can significantly increase its risk and potentially post negative absolute returns to the portfolio.

(A) hedging techniques
(B) rebalancing
(C) investment limits
(D) explicit leverage
(E) implicit leverage

6 _____ provides funds for use in product development and marketing for companies which have not yet sold their products commercially.

(A) Seed capital
(B) Other early stage financing
(C) Start up financing
(D) Secondary purchase financing
(E) Expansion financing

7 _____ practices focus on a company's social and environmental practices.

(A) SEE
(B) Corporate governance
(C) Dividend
(D) Private equity
(E) Venture capital

Answers to quizzes

Chapter 1   Managing portfolios

1   B.

2   D.

3   A.

4   E.

5   C.

6   D.

7   E.

Chapter 2   Portfolio theory

1   B.

Circumstance	Return	Probability	Expected return (px)	Deviation $(x - \bar{x})$	$p(x - \bar{x})^2$
I	10%	0.2	2.0	3.8	2.888
II	6%	0.5	3.0	−0.2	0.020
III	4%	0.3	1.2	−2.2	0.968
			$\bar{x} = 6.2$		Var = 3.876

Expected return = 6.2%

Standard deviation = $\sqrt{3.876}$ = 1.969%

2 C.

3 A.

Circumstance	Probability	$(x - \bar{x})$	$(y - \bar{y})$	$p(x - \bar{x})(y - \bar{y})$
I	0.2	−3.0	−1.5	0.225
II	0.5	+1.0	+0.8	0.400
III	0.3	+5.0	+2.5	3.750
			$COV_{xy} =$	4.375

Variance of x = 9.02
Variance of y = 2.30

$$r = \frac{COV_{xy}}{\sigma_x \sigma_y}$$

$$r = \frac{4.375}{\sqrt{9.02} \times \sqrt{2.30}} = 0.961, \text{ very high positive correlation}$$

4 B.

5 B.

The formula is $r_p = r_f + \beta(r_m - r_f)$
$r = 5 + 1.3(15 - 5) = 18\%$

6 E.

To review the formula:

$$\beta = \Sigma w_i \beta_i$$

where:

w_i = market value weighting of portfolio component i
β_i = the β of the portfolio constituent i.

Thus,

$$1.5 \times \frac{£100\,m}{£150\,m} + 0.8 \times \frac{£50\,m}{£150\,m} = 1.3$$

Chapter 3 Measuring returns

1 D.

Time-weighted return $= v_p = [(1 + v_1)(1 + v_2) \dots (1 + v_n)] - 1$

$\qquad\qquad\qquad\quad = [(1 + 0.05)(1 + 0.04)(1 + 0.03)] - 1$

$\qquad\qquad\qquad\quad = 1.12476 - 1$

$\qquad\qquad\qquad\quad = 12.48\%$ for the three-month period.

2 C.

The formula to use is:

$$R = \frac{(V_{end} - D) - V_{beginning}}{V_{beginning}}$$

Thus,

$$R = \frac{(70 - 5) - 60}{60} \times 100 = 8.33\%$$

3 E.

4 B.

5 A.

The benchmark portfolio is:

$B_1 = [0.60 \times \$100 \times (0.98)(1.03)] + [0.40 \times \$100 (1.05)(1.01)]$

$\quad = \$102\,984\,000$

The fund manager's performance versus the benchmark is:

$V_1 - B_1$

$= \$104\,000\,000 - \$102\,984\,000$

$= \$1\,016\,000$

The end of year value of the second benchmark portfolio is:

Value of B_2 (after first half of year)

$= [0.60 \times \$100 \times (0.98)] + [0.40 \times \$100 \times (1.05)]$

$= \$100\,800\,000$

Value of B_2 (after second half of year)

$= [0.40 \times \$100.8 \times (1.03)] + [0.60 \times \$100.8 \times (1.01)]$

$= \$102\,614\,400$

The value due to asset allocation is:

$B_2 - B_1$

$= \$102\,614\,400 - \$102\,984\,000$

$= -\$369\,600$

The value due to stock selection is:

$V_1 = B_2$

$= \$104\,000\,000 - \$102\,614\,000$

$= \$1\,386\,600$

6 A.

Fund	Return	Beta	Total risk
A	18%	1.20	17%
B	12%	1.05	15%

Sharpe measure $= \dfrac{R_p - R_f}{\sigma_p}$ Assume $R_f = 4.5\%$

Fund A $= \dfrac{18 - 4.5}{17} = 0.79$

Fund B $= \dfrac{12 - 4.5}{15} = 0.50$

We can conclude that using the Sharpe measure, fund manager A has outperformed fund manager B.

$$\text{Treynor measure} = \frac{R_p - R_f}{\beta_p}$$

$$\text{Fund A} = \frac{18 - 4.5}{1.20} = 11.25\%$$

$$\text{Fund B} = \frac{12 - 4.5}{1.05} = 7.14\%$$

Using the Treynor measure, we can conclude that fund manager A has outperformed fund manager B.

7 E.

Return from client's risk
The return from the client's desired portfolio is:

$$R_1 = 4.5 + 0.7 (5 - 4.5)$$
$$= 4.85\%$$

Thus, the return from the client's risk is:

$$(R_1 - R_f) = 4.85\% - 4.5\%$$
$$= 0.35\%$$

Return from market timing
The expected return on the actual portfolio is thus:

$$R_2 = 4.5 + 1.1 (5 - 4.5)$$
$$= 5.05\%$$

And this provides the return from market timing as:

$$(R_2 - R_1) = 5.05\% - 4.85\%$$
$$= 0.2\%$$

Return from selectivity
The return based on selectivity can be derived as:

$$(R_p - R_2) = 6\% - 5.05\%$$
$$= 0.95\%$$

Chapter 4 Indices

1 D.

Time period	Share price A	Share price B	Value of arith. index
0	100	100	100
1	90	105	97.5
2	85	120	102.5
3	70	125	97.5

The value of the index at time $0 = (100 + 100)/(100 + 100) \times 100 = 100$

The value of the index at time $1 = (90 + 115)/(100 + 100) \times 100 = 97.5$

The value of the index at time $2 = (85 + 120)/(100 + 100) \times 100 = 102.5$

The value of the index at time $3 = (70 + 125)/(100 + 100) \times 100 = 97.5$.

2 E.

Time period	Share price A	Share price B	Value of geom. index
0	100	100	100.00
1	90	105	97.21
2	85	120	101.00
3	70	125	93.54

Value of the geometric index at time $0 = \dfrac{\sqrt{(100 \times 100)}}{\sqrt{(100 \times 100)}} \times 100 = 100$

Value of the geometric index at time $1 = \dfrac{\sqrt{(90 \times 105)}}{\sqrt{(100 \times 100)}} \times 100 = 97.21$

Value of the geometric index at time $2 = \dfrac{\sqrt{(85 \times 120)}}{\sqrt{(100 \times 100)}} \times 100 = 101.00$

Value of the geometric index at time $3 = \dfrac{\sqrt{(70 \times 125)}}{\sqrt{(100 \times 100)}} \times 100 = 93.54$.

After time 2 the index value is 101.00.

3 A.

4 B.

Item	Base year		Current year	
	P_o (£)	Q_o	P_n (£)	Q_n
A	4.00	20	4.25	25
B	5.15	34	5.10	36
C	6.20	55	6.35	60
D	6.85	16	6.99	20

Item	P_nQ_n (£)	P_oQ_n (£)
A	106.25	100.00
B	183.60	185.40
C	381.00	372.00
D	139.80	137.00
	810.65	794.40

$$\text{Paasche index} = \frac{\Sigma P_nQ_n}{\Sigma P_oQ_n} \times \text{Base index value}$$

$$= \frac{810.65}{794.40} \times 100 = 102.05$$

5 A.

Item	P_nQ_o (£)	P_oQ_o (£)
A	85.00	80.00
B	173.40	175.10
C	349.25	341.00
D	111.84	109.60
	719.49	705.70

$$\text{Laspeyre index} = \frac{\Sigma P_nQ_o}{\Sigma P_oQ_o} \times \text{Base index value}$$

$$= \frac{719.49}{705.70} \times 100 = 101.95$$

6 A.

Chapter 5   Bond portfolio management

1 B.

2 E.

$$AF = \frac{(1 + r)^n - 1}{r}$$

$$= \frac{(1 + 0.08)^{16} - 1}{0.08} = 30.32$$

3 B.

4 D.

	Coupon amount	Discount 10%	Present value	PV × No. of years
1	15	0.9091	13.64	13.64
2	15	0.8264	12.40	24.79
3	15	0.7513	11.27	33.81
4	15	0.6830	10.25	40.98
5	15	0.6209	9.31	46.57
6	15	0.5645	8.47	50.80
7	15	0.5132	7.70	53.88
8	15	0.4665	7.00	55.98
9	15	0.4241	6.36	57.25
10	115	0.3855	44.34	443.37
			130.72	821.08
Macaulay duration				6.28
Modified duration				5.71

5 A.

Approximate change in bond price $= (-\text{Modified duration}) \times (\Delta y) \times (B)$

where:

Δy = change in yield

B = present value of the bond.

Using the example above, the calculation is:

$$\text{Change in bond price} = (-5.71) \times (0.001) \times (130.72)$$

$$= -0.75$$

Therefore, if the yield increases from 10.0% to 10.1%, the price of the bond will fall by about 0.75.

6 B.

7 C.

$$\text{Excess return to relative duration} = \frac{r_p - r_f}{d_p/d_m}$$

$$\text{Portfolio A} = \frac{20 - 4.5}{10/6} = 9.3$$

$$\text{Portfolio B} = \frac{10 - 4.5}{5/6} = 6.6$$

Chapter 6 Portfolio construction

1 D.

2 C.

3 A.

4 E.

5 B.

6 A.

$$\text{Forecast earnings per share} = \frac{\text{Forecast post-tax profit available to ordinary shareholders}}{\text{Number of shares issued}}$$

$$= \frac{£2 \text{ million } (1 - 0.33)}{10 \text{ million}} = 13.4\text{p per share}$$

$$\text{Forecast P/E ratio} = \frac{\text{Market price}}{\text{Forecast earnings per share}}$$

$$= \frac{201}{13.4} = 15$$

7 E.

Chapter 7   Types of analysis

1 E.

2 A.

3 E.

4 E.

5 B.

6 C.

7 A.

8 C.

Chapter 8   Valuation methodologies – shares

1 B.

$$V_0 = \frac{D_1}{(1+k)} + \frac{D_2}{(1+k)^2} + \frac{D_3}{(1+k)^3} + \ldots + \frac{D_t}{(1+k)^t}$$

Thus:

$$V_0 = \frac{\$50}{(1.10)} + \frac{\$50}{(1.10)^2} + \frac{\$50}{(1.10)^3} + \frac{\$50}{(1.10)^4}$$

$$= \$159.34$$

2 D.

The formula for the constant dividend growth rate model is:

$$V_0 = \frac{D_0 (1 + g)}{k - g} \left[1 - \left(\frac{1 + g}{1 + k} \right)^t \right]$$

where g does not equal k.

Plugging in the numbers from the question, the result is:

$$V_0 = \frac{80p (1.05)}{0.08 - 0.05} \left[1 - \left(\frac{1.05}{1.08} \right)^{15} \right]$$

$$= 965p$$

3 E.

The constant perpetual growth model is calculated using the following formula:

$$V_0 = \frac{D_0 (1 + g)}{k - g}$$

Where g < k

Thus:

$$V_0 = \frac{\$15 (1.03)}{0.10 - 0.03}$$

$$= \$225$$

4 B.

The dividend payout is calculated as follows:

$$\frac{\$2.48}{\$3.00}$$

$$= 0.827 \text{ or } 82.7\%$$

Thus, the retention ratio is:

$1 - 0.827 = 0.173$, or 17.3%.

The company's sustainable growth rate is $0.173 \times 10\% = 1.73\%$.

Using this data in the perpetual growth model, the value for the share can be calculated:

$$\frac{\$2.48(1.0173)}{(0.70 - 0.0173)}$$

$$= \$47.87 \text{ or } \$48.$$

This value is less than the actual share price of $75, and thus the stock is deemed to be undervalued.

5 A.

The formula for the two-stage dividend growth model is:

$$V_0 = \frac{D_0 (1 + g)}{k - g} \left[1 - \left(\frac{1 + g_1}{1 + k} \right)^t \right] + \left(\frac{1 + g_1}{1 + k} \right)^t \frac{D_0(1 + g_2)}{k - g_2}$$

Thus:

$$V_0 = \frac{\$4(1.06)}{0.09 - 0.06} \left[1 - \left(\frac{1.06}{1.09} \right)^5 \right] + \left(\frac{1.06}{1.09} \right)^5 \frac{\$4(1.03)}{0.09 - 0.03}$$

$$= \$18.41 + \$59.72$$

$$= \$78.13$$

6 D.

With this information, it is possible to estimate next year's share price using each of the ratios as follows:

Using the P/E ratio:

Expected price $=$ Average P/E $\times$ Current earnings per share

$\times$ (1 + Average earnings growth rate)

$= 10.2 \times \$5.50 \times 1.150$

$= \$64.52$

Using the P/CF ratio

Expected price $=$ Average P/CF $\times$ Current cash flow per share

$\times$ (1 + Average cash flow growth rate)

$= 7.6 \times \$6.8 \times 1.13$

$= \$58.40$

Chapter 9 Financial statement analysis and financial ratios

1 B.

2 A.

$$\text{Current ratio} = \frac{\text{Current assets}}{\text{Current liabilities}}$$

Thus, Company Z's current ratio $= \dfrac{760}{290}$

$= 2.62$

3 E.

$$\text{Gross profit margin} = \frac{\text{Sales} - \text{Cost of goods sold}}{\text{Sales}}$$

Thus, Company Z's gross profit margin for this year $= \dfrac{100 - 30}{100}$

$= 70\%$

Company Z's gross profit margin for last year $= \dfrac{90 - 25}{90}$

$= 72\%$

4 C.

$$\text{Return on stockholder's equity} = \frac{\text{Profits after taxes}}{\text{Total stockholder's equity}}$$

Thus the return on stockholder's investment in Company Z this year

$$= \frac{49}{870}$$

$$= 5.6\%$$

5 A.

$$\text{Dividend payout ratio} = \frac{\text{Annual dividends}}{\text{After tax earnings}}$$

Thus, Company Z's dividend payout ratio for this year $= \dfrac{12}{49}$

$$= 24.5\%$$

Company Z's dividend payout ratio for last year $= \dfrac{11}{46}$

$$= 23.9\%$$

6 D.

First, calculate the estimate of next year's share price using the following formula:

$$\text{Expected price} = \text{Average P/E} \times \text{Current earnings per share} \\ \times (1 + \text{Average earnings growth rate})$$

Using the data in the question, the two expected prices are:

Stock X

Expected price $= 15 \times 6.7 \times 1.10$

Expected price $= 111$

Stock Y

Expected price $= 20 \times 5 \times 1.20$

Expected price $= 120$

Holding stock Y will be a better option.

Chapter 10   Types of funds explained

1 D.
2 B.
3 E.
4 D.
5 E.
6 C.
7 A.

Glossary

Accounting earnings   The earnings of a firm as reported on its income statement

Active portfolio strategy   An investment strategy which attempts to achieve portfolio outperformance by forecasting broad market trends and/or by identifying particular mispriced sectors or securities in a market

Advance–decline line   A measure that compares the number of stocks that rose with the number of stocks that fell

Alpha   The abnormal rate of return on a security in excess of what would be predicted by an equilibrium model like CAPM

Alternative investments   An investment universe consisting of investments outside of the traditional market investments of publicly traded debt, equity, and property, and including investments ranging from hedge funds and managed futures to venture capital and private equity

Analyst   An employee of a stockbroker/fund management company who researches the prospects of a sector or company to assess likely investment performance

Annuity   A payment of a fixed amount of money at regular intervals of time

Asset   Something owned by a business, institution, partnership, fund or individual that has monetary value

Asset allocation   The percentage allocation of an investor's total portfolio in different asset classes

Asset class   A broadly defined group of securities that have similar risk and return characteristics, e.g. equities, bonds, cash

Balance sheet   An accounting statement that shows the assets, liabilities and equity of a firm on a specific date

Bar chart   A graph showing price movements over time, with high, low, and closing prices

Benchmark   A pre-selected portfolio, based on an index or peer group, the performance of which is used to compare with the performance of a fund manager's portfolio

Beta   The measure of the systematic risk of a security; the tendency of a security's returns to respond to swings in the broad market

Blue chip   Shares in a large, well-established and well-regarded company

Bond   A long-term debt obligation

Book value   A company's assets minus its liabilities representing the amount of capital invested in a company through retained earnings and through stock issuance

Bottom up approach   A method of portfolio management that involves selecting securities based on the fundamental analysis of individual companies

Broker   A person who acts as an intermediary between a buyer or seller and the market

Budget deficit   The difference between government spending and government revenues

Call option   An option to buy a financial instrument or other commodity

Candlestick chart   A bar chart that includes the opening price as well as the high, low, and closing prices

Capital market line (CML)   The highest sloped line achievable on the expected return and standard deviation graph

Cash flow   The amount of money flowing in and out of a portfolio or company

Cash flow matching   A form of immunization, matching cash flows from a bond with an obligation

Cash flow statement   An accounting statement that shows the flow of cash through the firm

Certificate of deposits (CDs)   Tradable bank deposits

Chartist   An analyst who produces charts for use in technical analysis

Coincident economic indicators   Economic statistics that are supposed to move in tandem with the business cycle

Commercial paper Unsecured debt obligation of a company, normally with a maturity of less that one year and usually issued at a discount

Common stock A security representing part ownership of a company

Constant dividend growth rate model A variation of the dividend discount model which assumes that dividends will grow at a constant growth rate over a specified time period

Constant perpetual growth model A simplified version of the constant dividend growth rate model where dividends are expected to grow at a constant growth rate in perpetuity

Convexity A measure of the curvature of the bond's price–yield curve or the rate of change of the slope of the price–yield curve

Core-satellite strategy A strategy of investing where the core of investments within a fund are made in traditional products such as equity and bond funds and the satellite or smaller portion of the investments are made in alternative investments

Corporate governance The systems of controlling the corporation providing a framework through which shareholders are assured legal compliance

Correlation coefficient A statistic in which the covariance is scaled to a value between minus one (perfect negative correlation) and plus one (perfect positive correlation)

Cost of goods sold The direct cost attributable to producing the product sold by the firm

Coupon The fixed periodic interest paid on a bond

Covariance A measure of the degree to which returns on two risky assets move in tandem

Currency risk The risk of the value of an asset changing because of movements in currency exchange rates

Current account deficit The difference between imports and exports, including merchandise, services, and transfers such as foreign aid

Current yield The stated annual coupon payment divided by the current bond price

Dedication A form of immunization, matching cash flows from a bond portfolio with an obligation

Defined benefit pension fund A pension fund plan where the sponsor agrees to pay members of the scheme a pension equal to a predetermined percentage of his or her final salary subject to the number of years for which the contributor has worked; also known as a final salary scheme

Defined contribution pension fund   A pension fund plan where contributions are used to buy investments and it is the return on these investments that will determine the pension benefits; also known as money purchase scheme

Derivatives   Contracts such as options, futures and swaps whose price is derived form the price of underlying financial assets

Discount rate   The rate used to calculate the present value of future cash flows

Diversification   Spreading a portfolio over many investments to avoid excessive exposure to any one source of risk

Dividend   A non-contractual payment to shareholders made from a company's after-tax profits

Dividend discount model (DDM)   A stock valuation method that values a share as the sum of all its expected future dividend payments, with the dividends adjusted for risk and the time value of money.

Dividend payout ratio   The portion of earnings paid out as dividends

Dividend yield   The annual dividend per share divided by the company's share price (net if dividend excludes the related tax; gross if tax is included)

Divisor   A number used in price-weighted indices that is adjusted for security changes such as stock splits

Dow theory   A technical theory that attempts to discern long- and short-term trends in stock market prices

Duration   A measure of the average life of a bond, defined as the weighted average of the times until each payment is made, with weights proportional to the present value of the payment

Dynamic asset allocation (i) A method of portfolio management involving buying stock index put options when the market is rising and selling them if the market is falling in order to maintain the value of a portfolio at a certain level while maintaining the potential for higher returns. This strategy is also known as portfolio insurance or hedging.
(ii) A strategy where the asset mix is automatically adjusted in response to market changes

Earnings per share (EPS) Post-tax profits attributable to ordinary shareholders divided by the number of shares outstanding

Economic earnings   The real flow of cash that a company could pay out forever in the absence of any change in the firm's productive capacity

Efficient frontier   A graph representing a set of portfolios that maximize expected return at each level of portfolio risk

Emerging markets   Financial markets of developing countries

Equity   Ordinary shares in a company

Exchange Traded Funds (ETFs)   Index or sector funds that are listed on exchanges and trade like stocks

Expected return   The probability-weighted average of the possible outcomes

FIFO   The first-in first-out accounting method of inventory valuation

Fiscal policy   Taxation and spending policies by a government designed to achieve GDP growth, relatively full employment, and stable prices

Fixed income security   A financial instrument, such as a bond, which pays a fixed rate of interest

Free cash flow stock valuation approach   An approach to valuing stocks that assumes that the intrinsic value of the equity in a firm is the present value of the net cash flows to shareholders that can be created by the company's existing asset base plus the net present value of investments that will be made in the future

Fundamental analysis   Detailed analysis of all relevant factors that are likely to influence the performance of an economy, sector or company, with a view to assessing investment prospects

Fund management   See portfolio management

Fund of funds   A fund that invests in a portfolio of other funds such as hedge funds

Futures contract   A negotiable contract to buy or sell standardized amounts of a financial instrument (or other commodity) at a fixed future date

General administrative expenses   The overhead expenses, including salaries, advertising and other costs, that are not directly related to production

Gilt   UK government debt obligation

Gross Domestic Product (GDP)   The total of goods and services produced in an economy

Gross redemption yield   A measure of the average rate of return that will be earned on a bond if held to maturity

Hedge fund An absolute return vehicle managed by entrepreneurial managers, which aims to achieve the highest return for a given level of risk

Hedging Limiting or reducing risk by buying an asset, usually a derivative, so that any losses can be offset by corresponding gains

Horizon analysis Interest rate forecasting that uses a forecast yield curve to predict bond prices

IFA An independent financial adviser

Immunization A strategy that matches durations of assets and liabilities so as to make net worth unaffected by interest rate movements

Income statement An accounting statement showing the flow of sales, expenses and earnings during a specified period

Index A number calculated by weighting a number of prices or rates for a selected set of assets according to a set of predetermined rules, e.g. the S&P 500. The purpose of the index is to provide a single number that represents the market movement of the class of assets it represents.

Index matching A category of portfolio management where a fund manager attempts to match the selected index as closely as possible and keep the fund positioned in this way as money flows in and out of the fund

Index staleness A situation occurring when stocks do not trade every day, and thus the index will not necessarily reflect all current stock price information

Indifference curve A curve connecting all portfolios with the same utility according to their means and standard deviations

Industrial activity A narrower measure of economic activity than GDP that focuses only on the manufacturing side of the economy

Inflation The rate at which general prices of goods in an economy rises

Information ratio A measure that explicitly relates the degree by which an investment has beaten a benchmark to the consistency with which the investment has beaten that same benchmark

Institutional investors Firms, such as insurance companies, pension fund and fund management companies, that invest in assets

Insurance company A company that accepts a certain risk in return for a payment of premium and agrees to make a payment if a certain event occurs

Investment styles Categorizations that imply that a fund invests in a distinct group of stocks that have some characteristics in common

Investment trust A company (closed end, i.e. with a fixed number of shares) which invests in the equities of other companies

Jensen measure The alpha of an investment

Lagging economic indicators Economic statistics that are supposed to move behind the business cycle

Laspeyre index A base-period quantity-weighted index

Leading economic indicators Economic statistics that are supposed to move ahead of the business cycle

Leverage The practice of borrowing to add to an investment position when it is believed that the return from the position will exceed the cost of borrowed funds

Leverage ratios Accounting ratios that indicate the financial risk of a firm by evaluating the firm's ability to pay its debt obligations

Liquidity ratios Accounting ratios that measure the ability of the firm to pay its immediate liabilities

Macauley duration A measure of the average life of a bond, defined as the weighted average of the times until each payment is made, with weights proportional to the present value of the payment

Managed futures An investment strategy that invests in listed financial and commodity futures markets and currency markets around the world

Management fee A fee collected by the manager that typically offsets any fund expenses

Market breadth indicators Technical indicators that measure the overall market strength or weakness

Market capitalization A share's price multiplied by all shares outstanding

Market value weighted index An index of a group of securities computed by calculating a weighted average of the returns of each security in the index, with weights proportional to outstanding market value

Maturity date The date on which a bond is due to be redeemed

Mezzanine debt Debt that incorporates equity-based options, such as warrants, with a lower-priority debt

Modified duration A measure utilized to approximate the change in a bond's price given a small change in the required yield

Monetary policy Actions by a central bank to control the supply of money and interest rates that directly influence the financial markets

Money market   A market for trading short-term debt, with a maturity of less than one year

Money-weighted returns   A technique that discounts the cash flow for each sub-period at an interest rate (the internal rate of return), which makes the sum of the present values of the cash flows and value of the portfolio at the end equal to the portfolio value at the beginning of the period

Moving average   A method of averaging the most recent past price data

Mutual fund   A managed pool of money invested in securities

Net asset value (NAV)   The current market value of securities in a fund, less liabilities on a per share basis; intrinsic value of a mutual fund

Net asset value per share   Net asset value divided by the number of shares in issue (or units for unit trust which is then equal to the unit price)

Net assets   The difference between a company's total assets and total liabilities, as shown in its balance sheet

OEIC   Open Ended Investment Company

Open-ended investment company (OEIC)   An investment company which operates in a very similar way to a unit trust, except that the Open Ended Investment Company is a legally constituted limited company. OEICs are not trusts and thus do not have a trustee; however, they have a depositary which holds the securities and has similar duties to a unit trust trustee.

Option   The right but not the obligation to buy or sell an asset or share

Option contract   A legal contract that gives its holder the right to buy or sell a specified amount of an underlying asset at a fixed price

Ordinary shares   Shares that give the rights of ownership in a company, such as voting or sharing in profits through dividends

Paasche index   A current-period quantity-weighted index

Par value   The maturity value of a bond

Passive portfolio strategy   A strategy of selecting stocks to match a pre-selected index or portfolio, with minimal analysis or input by the fund manager

Pension fund   A fund established to pay pension benefits to the beneficiaries once they retire

Performance attribution   The process of segregating the performance associated with asset allocation and with stock selection

Performance evaluation The process of measuring a fund manager's performance against a chosen benchmark and then assessing how the performance was actually achieved

Point-and-figure chart A graph with *x*'s and *o*'s used to plot price reversals without consideration of time

Portfolio A collection of assets

Portfolio management The process of combining securities in a portfolio tailored to the investor's preferences and needs, monitoring that portfolio, and evaluating its performance

Portfolio tilting A portfolio management strategy that combines elements of both passive and active fund management; for example, a fund manager might hold all the constituents of a particular index primarily in proportion to their market value, but may go overweight in certain sectors

Present value The current value of a future amount, calculated by discounting the future value by a specific rate of interest

Price to book ratio (P/B) The ratio of a company's stock price divided by the book value of the equity

Price to cash flow ratio (P/CF) The ratio of a company's stock price divided by the annual cash flow per share

Price to earnings ratio ('P/E ratio') A company's share price divided by its earnings per share. It is a relative measure of whether or not or a share is cheap or expensive.

Price to sales ratio (P/S) The ratio of a company's stock price divided by the company's current or most recent annual sales revenue per share figure

Private equity Investments in securities which are not publicly traded, usually in a private company

Profitability ratios Accounting ratios that measure the firm's earning potential

Profit and loss statement See income statement

Proprietary trading The use by a bank or financial institution of its own capital in the financial markets (usually bond or derivatives markets) in order to generate dealing profits

Put/call ratio A measure based on the volume of put and call option trading

Put option An option to sell a financial instrument or other commodity

Rebalancing Realigning the proportions of assets in a portfolio as needed

Relative strength indicator (RSI)   Measures the relative internal strength of a price pattern and is a percentage ranging from 0 to 100

Resistance   An upper bound on prices due to the quantity of willing sellers at that price level

Retained earnings   The portion of earnings retained within the firm for reinvestment or for future payouts

Return on equity (ROE)   An accounting term of net income divided by equity

Riding the yield curve   Buying long-term bonds in anticipation of capital gains as yields fall with the declining maturity of the bonds

Risk   Exposure to uncertain change, either positive or negative; when more than one possible outcome can occur

Risk-adjusted return   Investment performance adjusted for the level of risk that the strategy is exposed to

Risk-free asset   An asset with a certain rate of return; often taken to be short-term bills

Risk-free rate   The interest rate that can be earned with certainty

Risk premium   An expected return in excess of that on risk-free securities providing compensation for the risk of the investment

Security   A tradable financial instrument

Security market line   A graphical representation of the expected return – beta relationship of the CAPM

SEE   A company's practices relating to social, ethical, and environmental issues

Sentiment indicators   Indicators that attempt to gauge the overall mood and prevailing psychology of the general marketplace

Share   See common stock

Sharpe measure   A reward-to-volatility ratio; ratio of portfolio's excess return to standard deviation

Standard deviation   The square root of the variance; a statistical measurement of the dispersion about a fund's average return over a specified time period that describes how widely returns vary over the designated period

Statement of sources and uses of funds   See cash flow statement

Stock selection   An active portfolio management technique that focuses on advantageous selection of particular stocks rather than on broad asset allocation decisions

Style rotation   Switching from one investment style to another within the same portfolio

Support   A lower bound on prices due to the quantity of willing buyers at that price level

Systematic risk   Risk factors common to the whole economy; non-diversifiable risk

Tactical asset allocation   A method of portfolio management involving measuring the likely return on each asset class, using suitable measures, and then shifting more funds into the asset class which is expected to outperform

Technical analysis   Using detailed analysis of past price behaviour of shares (usually with charts) to predict future price movements

Time-weighted return   A measure of the compound growth rate of the value of the portfolio between any cash flow dates

Top down   An active portfolio management strategy that involves using fundamental analysis of economies and sectors in order to select the assets, regions or sectors that will result in the best investment return

Top down approach   A security selection approach for portfolios that starts first with the asset allocation and works systematically through sector and industry allocation to individual security selection

Total risk   Systematic risk plus unsystematic risk

Tracker funds   Funds that closely match a selected index

Tracking error   A measure that indicates the degree to which a manager deviates from the index returns

Treasury bill   Short-term, highly liquid government securities issued at a discount from the face value and returning the face amount at maturity

Trend line   A line drawn on a chart to identify current trends

Treynor measure   A ratio of excess return to beta

Two-stage dividend growth model   A version of the dividend growth model which assumes that dividends at a company first grow at one rate and then at another rate

Unemployment rate   The percentage of the labour force that is actively looking for work

Unit trust   An open-ended fund constituted under a Trust Deed between a fund manager and a trustee, in which investors buy units representing their proportional share of the assets and income of the trust

Unsystematic risk   Risk attributable to firm-specific risk or non-market risk

Utility value   The welfare a given investor assigns to an investment with a particular return and risk

Variance   A measure of risk or the dispersion around the mean

Venture capital   An investment in a start-up business that is perceived to have excellent growth prospects but does not have access to capital markets. It is a type of financing sought by new companies seeking to grow rapidly, in which cash is usually exchanged for equity.

Yield curve   A graph of yield to maturity as a function of time to maturity

Yield to maturity   A measure of the average rate of return that will be earned on a bond if held to maturity

Zero coupon bond   A bond that pays no interest and trades at a discount

Bibliography

Acharya, S. (2002) *Asset Management: Equities Demystified*. John Wiley & Sons Ltd.

Alexander, G. J., Sharpe, W. F. and Bailey, J. V. (2000) *Fundamentals of Investments*, 3rd edn. Prentice Hall.

Bodie, Z., Kane, A. and Marcus, A. J. (1999) *Investments*, 4th edn. Irwin/McGraw-Hill.

Bogle, J. C. (1999) *Common Sense on Mutual Funds*. John Wiley & Sons Ltd.

Choudhry, M. (1999) *An Introduction to Value-at-Risk*. Securities Institute (Services) Ltd.

Corrado, C. J. and Jordan, B. D. (2000) *Fundamentals of Investments (Valuation and Management)*. The McGraw-Hill Companies Inc.

Dimson, E., Marsh, P., Staunton, M. (2002) *Triumph of the Optimists, 101 Years of Global Investment Returns*. Princeton University Press.

Fabozzi, F. J. (ed.) (1998) *Active Equity Portfolio Management*. Frank J. Fabozzi Associates.

Fabozzi, F. J. (1999) *Investment Management*, 2nd edn. Prentice Hall.

Fabozzi, F. J. (ed.) (2000) *The Handbook of Fixed Income Securities*. McGraw-Hill.

Farrell, J. L. Jr (1997) *Portfolio Management Theory and Application*. McGraw-Hill.

Financial Training Company, The (1995) *Investment Management Certificate Study Course*.

Gitman, L. J. and Joehnk, M. D. (1998) *Fundamentals of Investing*. Addison Wesley.

Hills, R. (1996) *Hedge Funds (An Introduction to Skill Based Investment Strategies)* Rushmere Wynne Limited.

Hirschey, M. (2001) *Investments: Theory and Application*. Harcourt Inc.

Hyperion Training Ltd (1994) *Investment Management Certificate (IMC) Handbook*.

IIMR Investment Management Certificate Training Manual, 3rd edn.

Levy, H. (1996) *Introduction to Investments*. South-Western College Publishing, International Thomson Publishing.

Sharpe, W. (2000) *Portfolio Theory and Capital Markets*. McGraw-Hill.

Stoakes, C. and Freeman, A. (eds) (1989) *Managing Global Portfolios*. Euromoney Publications.

Index

Printed and bound by CPI Group (UK) Ltd, Croydon, CR0 4YY

08/05/2025

01864777-0001